Pastor Fran
+ D

She Can't
Even Play
the Piano!

We love and
appreciate
you!

God bless
Joyce

D0802876

She Can't Even Play the Piano!

Insights for Ministry Wives

Compiled by JOYCE WILLIAMS

Beacon Hill Press of Kansas City

Kansas City, Missouri

Copyright 2005
by Joyce Williams and Beacon Hill Press of Kansas City

ISBN 083-412-2006

Printed in the
United States of America

Cover Design: Paul Franitza

All Scripture quotations not otherwise designated are from the *Holy Bible, New International Version®* (NIV®). Copyright © 1973, 1978, 1984 by International Bible Society. Used by permission of Zondervan Publishing House. All rights reserved.

Permission to quote from the following additional copyrighted versions of the Bible is acknowledged with appreciation:

The Jerusalem Bible (JB), copyright © 1966 by Darton, Longman & Todd, Ltd., and Doubleday, a division of Bantam Doubleday Dell Publishing Group, Inc.

The *New American Standard Bible®* (NASB®), © copyright The Lockman Foundation 1960, 1962, 1963, 1968, 1971, 1972, 1973, 1975, 1977, 1995.

The *New King James Version* (NKJV). Copyright © 1979, 1980, 1982 Thomas Nelson, Inc.

The *Holy Bible, New Living Translation* (NLT), copyright © 1996. Used by permission of Tyndale House Publishers, Inc., Wheaton, IL 60189. All rights reserved.

Scripture quotations marked KJV are from the King James Version.

Library of Congress Cataloging-in-Publication Data

She can't even play the piano! : insights for ministry wives / compiled by Joyce Williams.
   p. cm.
  ISBN 0-8341-2200-6 (pbk.)
  1. Spouses of clergy—Religious life. 2. Christian women—Religious life. I. Williams, Joyce, 1944-

  BV4395.S48 2005
  253' .22—dc22

                   2004025751

10 9 8 7 6 5 4 3 2 1

Dedicated to the Memory of Bettye Williams

I never met my husband's first wife. And although it might seem just a little bit weird, I must say that I have come to love Bettye Williams and cherish her memory. She left a great legacy, and I've inherited the benefits of her wonderful, godly life in many ways. She surely could have written this book, because she had so much to share.

From all accounts, Bettye was the ultimate ministry wife. During her 39 years as Gene's wife, she unfailingly did whatever needed to be done. During their impoverished early seminary years, they lived in one room on a back porch, cooked on a hot plate, and shared a bathroom with other boarders. Bettye took in laundry, babysat, and typed term papers for other students to earn money while caring for their two babies.

During those seminary years Gene pastored a country church that stood in the middle of a Missouri wheat field. Each Sunday morning they got up before dawn and drove for more than an hour. Following the Sunday morning services, they spent the afternoons visiting in church members' homes. After the evening service, they packed up the boys and headed back to Kansas City.

Bettye played the piano (I can't!) and later learned to play the organ. Although she was unnerved at the thought of speaking before a group, she was a gifted Sunday School and Bible study teacher. Her class grew to more than 100 members, and the class remains a large, active one today. Gene said she always carried mints with her because her nervousness caused her mouth to be dry.

Bettye had a great sense of humor. I've been regaled with stories of how she loved to have fun. Once she introduced a pet snake to bridal shower guests in her home just to make things a little more exciting.

Bettye knew how to make people feel comfortable and important. In her special way she reached out to everyone around her with genuine love and concern.

The people in the churches Gene and Bettye pastored loved her. Gene likes to tell the story of being called to the Princeton, Florida, Church of the Nazarene. When the district superintendent notified him of the vote, he told Gene, "The church has called Bettye to be the pastor's wife." Gene hesitated a moment and then asked, "Does that mean I get to come too?"

Bettye was a dedicated wife and mother as well as an incredible cook. There just didn't seem to be anything she was not willing and able to do. She thrived in the scrutiny of fishbowl living and truly personified the Prov. 31 woman. Her five children and their children rise up and call her blessed. Bettye's sudden and untimely death in January 1991 ripped an enormous hole in the lives of everyone who knew her. They tell me her funeral procession was a mile long. Her memory is permanently etched on the hearts of everyone who knew her.

It is with great love and gratitude that I dedicate this book to the memory of one of the greatest pastor's wives who ever lived—Bettye Williams.

Contents

Foreword

Until Beverley came along, my real-life example of a pastor's wife was my mom. She often made 100 personal visits a week to shut-ins, folks in the hospital, members of the large adult Sunday School class she taught, and kids who rode the church bus to Sunday School. My mom was really something. She was of the generation of ministry who, although well-meaning, often put church before family and sometimes before personal concerns.

Beverley and I met when she was 18 and a freshman in college. I fell pretty hard, and before you could say "wedding day," we were married. She was barely 19, and I had reached the ripe old age of 20. The one thing we really had in common, other than loving each other, was that neither one of us wanted to go into ministry. In fact, that was the last thing we envisioned. But alas, with our first baby in tow, we arrived at seminary—a very unlikely couple in a pretty terrifying environment.

That's all a distant memory now. We have 31 years of shared pastoral ministry on the books and more than a decade of serving the greater Church as pastor to pastors. There are a lot of things we would just as soon not experience again, but we are what we are today because of our time serving the Body of Christ. It's been a wonderful journey.

I'm convinced by my personal experience that every man in ministry needs the dynamic love and affirmation of his wife. In our book *Married to a Pastor*, Neil Wiseman and I use a quote from Mrs. Norman Vincent Peale:

I agree that any woman might have other stimulating

jobs, but none is so difficult and demanding, so exciting and potentially rewarding as the job of living with a man, studying him, supporting him, liberating his strength, compensating for his weaknesses, making his whole being sing and soar the way it was designed to do (Ruth S. Peale, *The Adventure of Being a Wife* [Englewood, N.J.: Prentice-Hall, 1971], 2).

Those who live and serve in ministry marriages know how much a male pastor depends on his spouse for encouragement, validation of his work, and challenge of the mistaken assumptions he makes about himself and others. Yet there's another dimension to a shared ministry that's often overlooked—the distinct needs of the pastor's wife.

As I work with clergy couples in my role at Focus on the Family, it's clear that not all is smiles and fulfillment at home. We hear from pastors' wives who are frustrated, angry, and disillusioned. We also hear from many who find their roles as clergy wives exciting and rewarding.

Yet if I were to compile a laundry list of the concerns I hear from pastors' spouses, it would include loneliness, isolation, time pressures, insecurity, and issues related to raising children in the parsonage environment. I can't ease all these concerns, but I feel that throughout the pages of this book you'll find affirmation and encouragement.

I'm convinced that both the pastor and his wife need affirmation and encouragement. In a recent *Pastor's Weekly Briefing* column, I wrote, "Pastor, have you taken time lately to thank your partner in ministry for being so supportive? Have you attempted to help your spouse find fulfillment in recognizing and using his or her best gifts rather than simply handling obligatory chores as demanded by the expectations of the people in the pew?" (Adapted from *The Pastor's Weekly Briefing* 12:32 [Aug. 6, 2004]).

Unfortunately, and even unfairly, the impression you make

on a congregation can greatly impact the effectiveness of your husband's ministry. That's why the two of you should constitute a mutual admiration society to encourage one another, to be honest and speak the truth in love, and to be vigilant and guard against the dangers that might sabotage your relationship with each other and the effectiveness of your ministry. Most of all, it's important that you pray for one another—if not together, then separately. There's nothing more disappointing than a powerless, tepid ministry. Power comes from the prayers you offer on behalf of one another.

As I look through the pages of *She Can't Even Play the Piano! Insights for Ministry Wives*, I'm heartened by what I read from those who contributed to this book. I salute Joyce Williams for her courageous and tenacious determination to put an arm around clergy wives and, in so doing, lift a bit of the load of responsibility. Her book pours sunshine onto one of the most important roles in the Church of Jesus Christ— that of the pastor's wife.

—H. B. London Jr.

Introduction

"So what do you do? You don't sing. You don't preach or teach Sunday School. You can't even play the piano! What on earth do you do?"

I looked deeply into the face of the young Irish pastor's wife as she recounted this interchange with a parishioner at their first little church. Gene and I stayed with Pastor Ken White and his wife, Lynda, in their home in Bangor, North Ireland, for a week several years ago. We were traveling throughout Scotland, Ireland, and northern England for a month, speaking in many churches and encouraging pastors and their families.

As Lynda continued, I was happy to see a twinkle in her eyes as she said, "I told him, 'I love God and my husband. I take care of our three young children. I listen to our people when they need to talk. And I work two jobs so that my husband can afford to be a pastor!'"

I replied, "Go, girl! Good for you!"

"Just what do you do?" is an age-old, burning question for a ministry wife. What is her role? Some seem to do too much, and some are not involved enough. Can she satisfy everyone? Frankly, no—she can't. Even Jesus was disliked by many of the people He encountered. The unrealistic expectations that are imposed on wives in ministry can distress, depress, and destroy much of the joy of working for the Lord. The devil dances with glee when a pastoral team's effectiveness is diminished because of the wounded wife's pain and unhappiness resulting from painful encounters. It really is true: "If Mama ain't happy, ain't nobody happy!"

Overcoming stereotypical expectations has always been a

challenge. I once served on a church board that was searching for a new pastor. During one interview that I remember, predictably—and despite the candidate's philosophy of ministry, education, or calling—one board member asked the candidate the inevitable question "Does your wife play the piano?" That was a major factor for him.

So what is a ministry wife to do? How can she draw boundaries and prepare for the challenges that will come? Is it possible to find a balance that will work?

Frankly, I don't have the experience and credibility to address this issue with authority since I became a pastor's wife in my "middle ages." I missed many of the dynamics and challenges of being a young rookie pastor's wife. That's why I have called on some women who are seasoned ministry-wife veterans. Together they have experienced more than 1,000 years in ministry and have encountered just about every situation. You'll be hearing from them throughout the pages of this book.

It's true that every profession or calling has its own set of rewards and obstacles. For example, I can't imagine being married to a politician. My dear friend Vicki Tiahrt talks to me about the challenge of juggling all the schedules, managing homes in both Kansas and Washington, D.C., and being available to support her husband. Can you imagine campaigning and the rigors of reelections? (And you thought church votes were stressful!) Yet her husband, Congressman Todd Tiahrt, sings her praises everywhere he goes. He's known by many as simply "Vicki's husband." She attributes the balance she's sustained to her deep-rooted faith and constant communication with the Lord and is one of the most grounded and godly women I've ever met. (Read Vicki Tiahrt's testimony in my previous book *Unshakable Faith for Shaky Times*.) I'm convinced that rock-solid faith in God is the key to finding His path for us through the good times and the not-so-good times.

Some of the contributors to this book have conflicting

ideas on how to deal with certain issues. I believe that's a good thing. Each one of us brings a unique package designed by our Creator, and we bring different personalities and responses to various situations. The purpose of this book is to share insights from veteran ministry wives. Read their words, but listen to your Creator as you respond to the myriad challenges of living in the fishbowl of ministry life.

My prayer is that your ministry will be a rewarding journey of joy around the quagmires and quicksand that await you. May each of you be encouraged and uplifted by the testimonials and insights shared by these veterans. Then, when that inevitable question comes, "Just what do you do?" you can respond with candor and humor.

Even if you can't play the piano!

Preserving Proper Priorities

"I can't do this anymore!"

Susan's frantic cry riveted my attention. The young pastor's wife anxiously watched her toddler run through the house as the baby began to cry in the next room. I had stopped by to give a book to her and caught her in a manic ministerial mode. Susan went on: "I'm supposed to be at church in 45 minutes to help with this week's Bible study. I was loading the car and was just about ready to leave when the phone rang. It was one of our members who was in crisis and needed to talk. My husband beeped into the call to ask me to bring some things to him when I come to church. I finally got off the phone, gathered my husband's items, and was headed to the car when the baby threw up all over himself. I was just getting ready to change his clothes when the doorbell rang. What am I going to do?"

That's not an untypical parsonage scene. Very rarely do things go as planned or according to schedule. How do we juggle the pressures and responsibilities? Can we be all things to all people? Absolutely not. Then how do we draw proper and godly boundaries?

The demands on Kay Warren and her husband, Rick, with their huge congregation at Saddleback Church in Lake Forest,

California, and their diverse ministries are enormous. Read what Kay has to say about the pressure.

We laugh at the absurdity that any of us could ever be the perfect woman. But I know that most of us have had that dream. This can be especially true of ministry wives. Because of unrealistic expectations, many times we overcommit ourselves and become too busy.

There are some things that let me know when I'm too busy. My husband, Rick, will confirm that these are, I'm sorry to say, real examples from my life.

- You know you're too busy when you have not emptied your mailbox in three days.
- You know you're too busy when you walk in the door and the dog growls at you because he doesn't recognize you.
- You know you're too busy when you mumble, "To-morrow night, Honey," for a week.
- You know you're too busy when your pots and pans have cobwebs on them.
- You know you're too busy when the guy at the drive-through window at Taco Bell knows you so well he's willing to loan you money.
- You know you're too busy when your microwave prints a personal "Hi, Kay!" message on the screen.
- You know you're too busy when you use your bathtub as a planter.
- You know you're too busy when you stop shaving your legs—it just takes too much time.

The list could go on and on. The truth is that damage results from overloaded lives. Almost all women today (particularly ministry wives) feel guilty because we can't do it all or be all things to all people. Some might say, "I'm OK with my career, but my health is falling apart." Others might say, "I'm doing OK as a mom, but my marriage is falling apart." The part that's not OK can become very destructive.

As ministry wives we can say, "I'll do whatever it takes to find margin, to build balance, and to stop the overload that has been so destructive and damaging. Simply pray, saying, *God, whatever it takes, I'm willing to do or not do that. I'm willing to do whatever it is You reveal to me the rest of this day, the rest of this week— whatever it takes, God. I'm willing to make changes, because I want what You've promised—life to the fullest.*

Then as ministry wives we'll be able to begin to experience what He has for us as we begin to delight our hearts in Him.

—Kay Warren

Most ministry wives can relate to Kay's list. Each of us would certainly agree with her that there are not enough hours in the day to accomplish all that we need to do. Some guidelines on how to complete those necessary assignments and yet reserve time with the Lord and for ourselves could include these:

- Get organized and into a routine. For example, plan menus for future meals as much as possible.
- Make time for fun.
- If you're a morning person, set the alarm clock to sound 15 minutes earlier so that you can be sure to have your quiet time with the Lord.
- Try to set aside at least a one hour each week to pamper yourself.

She Can't Even Play the Piano!

Carol Rhoads served in pastoral ministry with her husband, Ross, for more than 20 years. Although she is one of the blessed ones who plays the piano beautifully, that ability did not exempt her from encountering some of the problems and issues that are common to ministry. She tells us about it:

Soon after I became a pastor's wife, I realized that some of the people had expectations of my role based on what the former pastors' wives had done. And they began to drop not-too-subtle hints: "Our former pastor's wife headed Vacation Bible School, another one taught the kids in the junior department, and our last pastor's wife had at least 20 people over for dinner every Sunday night." I felt overwhelmed.

Our children had some identity problems as well. One of them asked, "If Daddy's called 'Pastor,' what should we call *you*?" Then they decided I should be "Mommy Pastor." The stress and pressure intensified, and I felt uncertain of my role. When I shared my concerns with Ross, his response was very reassuring. He said, "Honey, you're the pastor's wife, not the church's wife." That wise statement provided more freedom for me than can be imagined.

Many people assume that pastors meet their church members' needs before they respond to their own family's needs. Living in the glass walls of a parsonage was a constant challenge. I had to learn to balance the needs of church versus family. As our children grew and the church grew, the demands on me increased at home and at church. Ross encouraged me to seek God's wisdom concerning how I would divide my time and responsibilities. He never pressured me to do what was "expected."

Most pastors' wives are expected to attend prayer meeting, but there were many times when I sat at one of the children's ballgames instead. Because I love to play the piano, I enjoyed playing for most of the services—even when we began having three morning services. But it soon became too much for the children to wait through all three services. It was not hard for me to cut back on my schedule.

—Carol Rhoads

Hazel Mabe was not a ministry wife. She was a lady in my home church who taught me and others a lot about preserving proper priorities and doing what our Father asks us to do with the resources with which we are blessed.

No one ever guessed that the quiet little lady who lived so frugally would some day leave more than $1 million for world evangelism. Hazel Mabe was a quiet, unprepossessing lady who lived quite modestly. Her life demonstrated that her priorities were in divine order. Her faith in God was obvious.

For more than 50 years she drove to church every Sunday in her aging sedan and slipped unobtrusively into a pew near the back. We remember her ready smile and her expression of wide-eyed wonder.

I remember sitting behind Hazel Mabe in church one Sunday morning when I was a little girl. I was totally fascinated by the beauty of the fawn-colored velvet hat that was perched precisely on her head. I was especially intrigued with the colorful feather tucked into its band. Although I should have been listening to the preacher's message, I must confess that I was absorbed with the idea of stroking the soft velvet and smoothing that feathery plume.

Paradoxically, although she was very quiet, there were issues about which Hazel was strongly opinionated. She never hesitated to express her thoughts on certain topics and issues in which she believed. Because of her modesty very few people knew that she had attended Asbury College. She had keen insight and perception, and people listened when she talked.

For several years she taught the Junior Girls' Sunday School class. One of the fondest memories from Shirley, one of "her" girls, was a day trip to Natural Bridge. For many who lived in the church's inner-city neighborhood, it was a special outing that is still remembered.

Although she chose to live in an aging two story brick house on a busy corner, there's no doubt she could have moved out to a quieter, more affluent neighborhood. But she was perfectly content to stay right where she was and drive her old car.

Because, you see, Hazel Mabe had her heart set on property that was out of this world. Her investment strategy was to store up treasures in a place where moths and rust could not destroy them and where thieves could not break in and steal (Matt. 6:20). With that in mind, when she finalized her estate plans she indicated her heart's desire to leave her assets to the church to be used for the expansion of the kingdom. She wanted her faith to be perpetuated throughout the world.

Late Sunday evening, January 30, 1999, Wayne Dunman, stopped by his office on his way home from church. Since his office was across the street from where Hazel lived, he and his wife, Becky, had gotten in the habit of checking on Hazel. When he noticed that her drapes were still open and the lights were burning brightly, he immediately realized that something was wrong. He walked over to her house and knocked on the door. When there was no answer Wayne peeked in the window. To his dismay he saw her sitting slumped in her comfortable old chair. She had passed away.

How fitting to realize that on that Lord's Day Hazel had sat down for a nap and never awakened. It was as though the

Father said, "Come home, dear child. It's time for you to join your treasures. I have beautiful riches and wealth beyond measure to show you."

When her will was probated, properties liquidated, and her estate settled, a check in the amount of $1,214,000.00 was presented to Dr. Louie Bustle in a special service on May 6, 2001. She had stipulated that those funds be used to take the gospel around the world—especially to the poorest of the poor. Because of Hazel's heavenly investments, countless numbers will hear the gospel.

So many times we are tempted to collect feathers for our caps and garnish our works with grandiose gestures. Through her example Hazel Mabe is still teaching us life lessons. Don't store up our treasures here. Invest them so that dividends will compound for eternity. Live humbly, stand for what is right, and deposit your assets in the eternal vaults of heaven.

As beautiful and intriguing as that velvety, feathered hat from more than half of a century ago may have been, it is long gone. But on that blustery Sunday afternoon when Hazel closed her eyes for the last time she could have echoed Paul's words in 2 Tim. 4:6-8, ". . . The time has come for my departure. I have fought the good fight. I have finished the race. I have kept the faith. Now there is in store for me the crown of righteousness."

Hazel Mabe has received her reward. And it is a crown she will wear forever.

Many times our plans for our lives do not turn out the way we anticipate. Genell Johnson shares how thankful she is today for the riches the Lord has given her:

※

I was a pastor's kid who became a pastor's wife.
That certainly was not something I dreamed of or

planned for during high school and early college days. I remember telling my parents that I planned to marry a rich man—or at least a man whose income would be considerably more than my father's. But God had other plans.

During my sophomore year of college, I totally committed my life and future to God, and He cleansed my heart and filled me with His Holy Spirit. Before long, I realized that a certain redheaded religion major was becoming a very significant part of my life. Forget the rich-man plans. I knew what I was destined for—life in the parsonage.

My husband, Talmadge, and I served in the pastorate for 14 years in two very different but equally wonderful churches. Those were eventful, interesting, and blessed years. They were also years of learning that proved to be profitable, although sometimes painful.

If I were to share my experience as a pastor's wife in a neat, three-point summary, I would say something like this:

1. I learned early on that I could not be all things to all people. I tried during that first pastorate. I so wanted to be the perfect pastor's wife. I thought that I had to do all the things that the laypersons couldn't or wouldn't do. I expected more of myself than God did—and maybe more than some of the people. What a releasing discovery to learn one day that God just wanted me to love Him and serve the people by simply loving them!

2. I've always been rather open and expressive. Most of the time, this is a good thing; sometimes it's not so good. It was quite a revelation to learn at one of Florence Littauer's conferences that there is such a thing as a *sanguine* personality. That's me! I also

learned that we sanguines have our very own strengths and weaknesses. I knew through a painful experience involving a good church member-friend to guard my mouth—even in jesting. Words are hard to take back. Furthermore, not everyone is interested in my opinion— however good it might be. I still have to practice caution when it comes to expressing my views. Sometimes it's better to speak my mind at home or not at all.

3. After a few unpleasant and uncomfortable experiences, I finally learned that it's all right to say, "No, but thank you for asking." If you don't have the time or are uncomfortable with the request, it's OK to respectfully decline. I'm thankful that I came to realize my limitations. God has always helped me when I've needed Him to make the difference.

One of my favorite Scripture passages is Prov. 3:5-8, and it's great advice.

I've truly discovered that God is good—*all the time*!

—Genell Johnson

I'm sure all ministry wives would agree that it's essential to make a deliberate and concerted effort to preserve proper priorities. Our pastor's wife, Pam Morgan, shares her philosophy:

Each stage of my life has given me a different schedule with which to deal. Although I did not work full time when our children were young, I was very busy at home as well as supporting our ministry. So I learned to be selective in where I expended my time and energy. My first commitment was to my husband and our children.

She Can't Even Play the Piano!

I learned that the best thing I can do each day is to start out by asking the Lord to order my day so that I can see things from His perspective. That may mean that on some days I simply maintain things at home. On other days I was able to extend my ministry beyond my family. There have been times when I've found that interruptions to my schedule ended up being the most blessed or meaningful times of the day.

As a people-pleaser with the middle-child syndrome, I find myself always wanting to be happy and get along with everyone. So I've found balance in turning to God's Word, because ultimately I'll answer to the Lord. My desire must be to please Him above all else. I've made Ps. 19:14 my life prayer: "May the words of my mouth and the meditation of my heart be pleasing in your sight, O LORD, my Rock and my Redeemer."

—Pam Morgan

That verse would serve all of us well as a prayer for our lives. Even on the days Kay Warren mentioned when we don't have time to shave our legs, our pots and pans have cobwebs, and our bathtub is being used as a planter, we can still pray, *Father, since I can't possibly make everyone happy, I ask You to enable me to establish and sustain priorities that will please You and bring glory to Your name.* I agree with Genell Johnson, who loves Prov. 3:5-6: "Trust in the LORD with all your heart, and lean not on your own understanding; in all your ways acknowledge him, and he will make your paths straight." As He answers our prayer and fulfills His promises, He will clarify our priorities and enable us to maintain them daily.

Then maybe your dog will recognize you when you come home!

Raising Children While the Congregation Watches

Raising kids in the spotlight is a huge challenge for ministry families. Not long ago, a young pastor's wife, the mother of three children under the age of six years, told me, "Regardless of what my children do or don't do, somebody in the church has something negative to say about it. There's one lady in particular who feels it's her responsibility to tell me how to raise my kids. I know that she genuinely loves us and feels that she's only trying to help me, an inexperienced mother. I'm reluctant to respond too strongly, because her husband is not only the church treasurer but is also the chairman of the board of elders. This is our first assignment since seminary, and I really don't feel that I can take much more of this." Then she asked me, "What do you think I should do?"

To be totally honest with her, I had to respond, "She obviously has no right to criticize you and your children. Yet I realize your concern about antagonizing her." Then I said, "You know, during the few years I was a pastor's wife, all our children were grown. So I never had to deal with those issues." I referred her to a pastor's wife who had raised four children in the ministry spotlight.

Once again, I defer to the veterans who have been there. How do we Teflon-coat our children to keep them from being hurt? The old adage "An ounce of prevention beats a pound of cure" certainly works in ministry families. Beverley London shared great words of wisdom in my previous book with Beacon Hill Press, *Unshakable Faith for Shaky Times*:

You may often wonder how your children will remember and reflect on their lives under the microscope. That concerned us. But our two sons are doing great. In fact, both of them are involved in para-church type vocations and are happily married. They've blessed us with four beautiful and handsome grandchildren. Our family is a great source of satisfaction and thanksgiving.

What did we do as clergy parents? We loved them, affirmed them, prayed for them, and when it was time, we let them go. We didn't raise them as if they were the property of the church but as our precious children. We let them make their own life choices, provided parameters for their guidance, and taught them to respect the church, school, and authority. When they left for college, we prayed a prayer, shed a tear, took a deep breath, and trusted God with our sons and the decisions we had made. . . .

Please don't ever give up on your children. Don't ever let them feel that they're playing second fiddle to the congregations you serve. Whatever you do, pray for them every day. Then have faith enough to set them free. God *will* respond to you. That's His promise—not mine, but His! (Joyce Williams, comp., *Unshakable Faith for Shaky Times* [Kansas City: Beacon Hill Press of Kansas City], 131-32).

—Beverley London

Gene and I are blessed to have Paul and Oreta Burnham as dear friends. They have been missionaries and Bible translators to the Ibaloi Indians in the Philippines for more than 30 years. Their five children grew up in their ministry home. All of them stayed true to the Lord and became involved in ministry. Their son Martin was martyred after he and his wife, Gracia, spent more than 13 months as captives of rebel forces in the Philippines. (Martin and Gracia's story is recounted by Gracia and Oreta in my book *My Faith Still Holds*.) When Martin and Gracia were taken captive in May 2001, God was honored by their example to others and by their love for those who mistreated them. Martin was killed during a rescue attempt, but today his witness goes on. Many have accepted the challenge to become missionaries as a result of his testimony and life example.

It was a blessing to talk with Oreta about the joy of watching her children carry on the work of spreading the gospel. I asked her, "How did you do it? How were you and Paul able to bring up all of your children in such a healthy environment that they did not rebel and are serving the Lord today? How would you advise ministry wives today?" Here's her response:

She Can't Even Play the Piano!

Paul and I were in our early 30s when we began our service in the Philippines as church planters with New Tribes Mission with the Ibaloi Tribe. Our children Brian, Cheryl, Doug, and Martin ranged in age from 4 to 10 at that time. Felicia, our fifth child, was born in the Philippines. Some people thought we were unreasonable to raise our young children on the mission field. But we knew God's call was on our lives, and this was His plan for us. We had full confidence that He would guide us and give us wisdom to bring up our children with loving care—even under challenging circumstances.

What makes missionary parents different than others? Nothing really. We're the same as other Christian families, and we face the same struggles that many other parents do. We learned very early in our ministry that it was essential to let Christ know how we feel and seek His guidance in every situation as we raised our children and went about our daily work.

Some have commented to me that missionaries must be different. How could we face so many separations from our children and families and not be affected by it? To be honest, this can be done only by God's grace.

There are several ways we prepared for the challenges.

- We prayed for wisdom in raising our children even before they were born.
- We prayed for a godly home.
- We prayed that they would trust the Lord as personal Savior at an early age.
- Church attendance was a given.
- We taught them the basic principles in God's Word.
- Paul and I were active in our church with Sunday

School and Bible studies, and our children went with us.

When we went to the Philippines with New Tribes Mission, it became necessary to send the children to board at Faith Academy in Manila during the week. They came home each weekend their first year there. It was hard to send them off for five days each week, but the Lord had brought us to the Philippines to work with a tribal group, and boarding school was one of the sacrifices we had to make.

We missed the children's laughter and playing games and reading with them. Our days were busy learning the language and culture, but the evenings were long and lonely.

After that first year we got to see the children only once a month or so. We missed them so much, and they missed being at home. But we adjusted, because we knew it was God's plan for our lives.

The children had breaks for holidays as well as fall and spring breaks. We planned vacations together. But our favorite times were when they came home to the mountains. They always had their own rooms, and I think that was very important for them. They were full of things to tell us. They read books and played with their toys. Before long, all of them were together laughing and talking about school and their friends.

The children developed a great love for the tribal people. They saw the need and knew why we came to the Philippines. Their love for the country of the Philippines grew strong, and they saw that we were making a difference. They were proud and would call it "our work" since we told them they were a vital part of what God had called us to do.

We prayed for our children as the time drew near

for them to go to college and make many life decisions. We prayed specifically—

- that they would have a close walk with the Lord and be sensitive to His leading;
- that they would seek God's will for their lives, regardless of what it was. We knew that the Lord could use them;
- that the Lord would lead them to a godly lifetime mate in marriage;
- that they would not be led astray by things they would hear and see, since they would be returning to their home country where the lifestyle would be foreign to them.

I encourage you to

- pray for wisdom to raise your children to respect the Lord;
- pray that your children will trust the Lord as their Savior at an early age;
- be faithful to teach your children God's Word;
- protect your children from bad influences;
- live out your faith before them;
- make sure your children know they're loved and that they're a special part of the family;
- take time to show your children that you love them, to be interested in the things they do, and to have special times with them;
- teach your children that they can be witnesses for the Lord and that others are watching their lives;
- pray for godly Christian mates for your children;
- pray that your children will have a close walk with the Lord;
- continue to pray for your children as they serve the Lord and raise their families.

Parenting continues for the rest of our lives. The focus just changes as we continue to pray for our children and grandchildren throughout their lives.

—Oreta Burnham

So what is the key to raising godly children in a ministry family? I'm sure we can all agree that the most important element is to follow God's plan for our lives—wherever that takes us. Trust the Lord for guidance, and pray, pray, pray.

What Do We Do When Our Kids Stray?

Gene and I were speakers for a retreat for pastors and their spouses in New England. Everyone was smiling and wearing their "happy face" masks. During one of the sessions, as we began to share about lost lambs in ministry homes, a number of the facades began to crumble as walls of secrecy and isolation came down. One after another, participants stood and wept openly as they shared from broken hearts their concerns for their wayward children and grandchildren. We were deeply moved.

One pastor said, "We thought we did all the right things. We tried to be there for our son and to interact in his life while we did ministry. He's our only child, and he was a model son. He went off to a Christian college, met a beautiful girl, and got married right after graduation. He had a great job. Then he got involved in Internet pornography and had an affair with one of the women who worked in his office. When his wife found out, she packed up and left with our two grandchildren. Now an intense custody battle is going on." Between sobs, his wife said, "We're not sure we'll ever see out grandkids again."

The rising number of prodigals who come from ministry homes is alarming. Everywhere we go, it seems as though the enemy is attacking these families where they're most vulnerable—through their children. It's true that we never expected fair play from Satan, but it's hardest when we see our children led astray. Carol Cymbala knows about this problem.

I'd always worried about my three children attending public schools in New York, but there was no money to send them to private schools. Surprisingly, the problem didn't begin in school. It started in church. Right under our noses.

Our oldest, Chrissy, had gotten involved with some unhealthy influences at the Brooklyn Tabernacle. Gradually, we began to see a hardening of her heart toward us and toward God. She changed from the sweet, well-behaved youngster we had raised to someone we could hardly recognize. From where I stood, it seemed as though she was being destroyed in front of our eyes. I felt helpless as she spun out of control.

Despite our pleading, Chrissy remained hard as a rock. My husband did most of the talking with her but got absolutely nowhere. Yelling, crying, encouragement, gifts, and a change of location—we tried it all. But she wouldn't budge. Eventually Chrissy left home, which was something we never dreamed could happen. The more we prayed, the worse she seemed to get. On and on it went until the pain of it for a mother's heart became excruciating.

One Friday night as the choir began to pray before practice, I felt so attacked by Satan that I thought I was losing my mind. The pressure was so strong that I did the unthinkable and just walked out of practice. Then I made my way to a local department store where I sat for two hours in the furniture section sobbing my heart out.

That night, it seemed as though Satan was whispering an ugly threat to me. He had gotten hold of Chrissy, and he was going to devour Susan and James as well unless I got them out of New York. I loved my husband and I loved the choir and the work God had called us to. But I wasn't willing to sacrifice my children. I didn't know what to do.

I felt the weight of the last two years of Chrissy's rebellion pressing in on me. Had Jim and I overstayed our time in Brooklyn? Were we asking too much of ourselves and assuming it was God's will? If not, why had we lost our daughter? The questions kept swirling around me, eroding my faith. That was when I decided I had to do something. I wasn't going to lose my other two children the way I had lost Chrissy.

When I told Jim I was ready to pack my bags and leave with the other two kids, he was stunned. "Carol, we can't just leave without knowing what God wants us to do. He's called us here. We have to hold on until He gives us clear direction."

Somehow I managed to resist the temptation to run; I don't know how. But I had a hard time keeping my anxiety and depression under control.

Carol goes on to share about being diagnosed with cancer and having a hysterectomy during that time. She also is very transparent about the anguish and pain Chrissy's condition continued to cause for her and Jim.

⌒✿⌒

During my time of struggle, Jim was as broken up by Chrissy's condition as I was, but he reacted differently. At first he confided in some close friends, but after a few months he sensed God wanting him, as he says, "to stop crying, screaming, or talking to anyone else about Chrissy. I was to converse with no one but God." That meant keeping Chrissy at a distance too, and though it broke my heart that the two of them weren't talking to each other, I knew I had to respect his decision. One Tuesday night Jim headed to the prayer meeting, his heart still heavy with the knowledge that Chrissy was so far from God.

⌒✿⌒

Carol tells about a Tuesday-night prayer meeting when a young woman felt impressed to pray for Chrissy. So in place of their regular prayer time, they prayed specifically for Chrissy.

⌒✿⌒

It was almost as though the church experienced labor pains that night as they prayed God would bring our daughter from death to life. When Jim came home from the prayer meeting, he told me, "Carol, it's over."

"What's over?" I asked him.

"It's over with Chrissy. You would have had to be in the prayer meeting tonight to understand, but I tell you, if there's a God in heaven, this whole nightmare is finally over."

That evening, though we didn't know it, Chrissy was having her own nightmare. She woke up frightened by a terrible dream. In it, she could see herself heading toward a bottomless pit. She felt terrified, realizing her sin was leading her straight to hell. But as she dreamed, she also felt God holding her back from the edge and lifting her up. In the midst of her fear, He was telling her how much He loved her.

I could hardly believe it when I opened the door on Thursday morning and saw her standing there. She actually fell to her knees and began begging our forgiveness for how she had been living. I threw my arms around her, and we both burst into tears. I had my child back at last.

Our nightmare lasted two years. They had seemed the worst years of our lives, and I had nearly lost the struggle because of my fear for my children. But God had not abandoned us. Instead, He had shown His faithfulness in a marvelous way. And Chrissy's life was beginning all over again.

Carol and Jim remained faithful, and so did God. In the midst of her darkest hours, God gave Carol the beautiful song *He's Been Faithful:*

In my moment of fear
Through every pain, every tear
There's a God Who's been faithful to me.
When my strength was all gone,
When my heart had no song,
Still in love He's proved faithful to me;
Every word He's promised is true;
What I thought was impossible I see my God do.

She Can't Even Play the Piano!

When my heart looked away
The many times I could not pray
Still my God He was faithful to me.
The days I spent so selfishly,
Reaching out for what pleased me;
Even then God was faithful to me.
Every time I come back to Him,
He is waiting with open arms
And I see once again.

He's been faithful, faithful to me.
Looking back His loving mercy I see
Though in my heart I have questioned
Even failed to believe
Yet He's been faithful, faithful to me.

—Carol Cymbala

Taken from "He's Been Faithful" by Ann Spangler; Carol Cymbala. Copyright © 2001 by Carol Cymbala. Used by permission of The Zondervan Corporation.

Yes, there is hope for our lost lambs. Our faithful Father always gives us just what we need to give us hope. Here are some things that have worked for me and that I encourage you to do as well:

- Hold on to God's promises.
- Trust Him.
- Never give up on your kids.
- Pray and fast for your kids.
- Surrender your guilt and regrets.
- Don't anticipate tomorrow's tragedies.
- Become proactive.
- Enlist the prayers of friends. Develop a prayer strategy.
- Remember: your prayers will outlast you

Our friend H. B. London Jr. writes words of comfort to pastors and spouses in his book *Just Call Me Pastor:*

⌒ℳ⌒

I know some of you are grief stricken because your grown children are not serving the Lord. And so you suffer anguish when you see them ignore the faith values you taught them. You pray that they will not throw away the priceless treasures of their heritage. And so you lie awake going over what you might have done differently. You cry out in prayer during the night hours. . . . Your conscience haunts you. You didn't spend enough time with them. You didn't go to that basketball game you promised to attend. You neglected to read the Bible and pray with them as much as you should have. Take courage. There is hope. I want to remind every pastor and spouse that God is not through with your children. No matter how old they are, they are still *your* children. And you can still do some parenting. That quiet inner strength that only a stalwart Christian communicates has far more impact on them than you imagine. Rest in the knowledge that God is at work in their memories because of what they learned from you. Believe it, and feed your faith on that fact. Also remember that God has many ways to reach them in addition to what you can do. . . . So, dear parent, don't give up hope. Even if you go to be with the Lord before your children turn back to Him, He will keep tracking them down with His love.

—H. B. London Jr.

Taken from *Just Call Me Pastor,* by H. B. London Jr. Copyright © 2000 by H. B. London Jr. and Neil B. Wiseman, and Regal Books, Ventura, California.

Gene and I have been privileged to work with Stuart and Jill Briscoe on several occasions. Once when they were with us in our home, we discussed the heartbreak of lost lambs. Jill said, "Sometimes I think we get so bogged down praying for all the temporary crises and immediate problems that we neglect to pray for God's big thing in their lives—the purpose for which they were created." She went on to say, "I think we should focus on praying for the big thing." From personal experience I would certainly agree. Since that discussion, I've made a conscious effort to remember to pray for the fulfillment of God's purpose in our children and grandchildren's lives. After all, He has vowed to fight our battles for us. I love the precious promise found in Isa. 49:25: "I will contend with those who contend with you, and your children I will save." The Holy Spirit, the Hound of Heaven, is on the trails of our loved ones who have gone to the "far country." And He can go where we can't go, say what we can't say (or shouldn't), be what we can't be, and do what we can't do. He uses people, circumstances, situations, songs, and many other things in ways that are beyond our imaginations.

I shared this promise during a women's retreat in Pennsylvania a couple of years ago. The lady who prayed the closing prayer asked God to send the "hound dog of heaven" after our lost lambs. (I later asked her if she was an Elvis fan!) I love that concept. Obviously, God is a gentleman and never forces himself upon us. What that promise means to me is that our Father will continue to send the Holy Spirit to constantly seek to draw our precious lambs back into the fold regardless of how deeply into the "far country" they may wander. Although their final answer is their choice, I am assured that as long as they live, our lambs will be pursued by the Hound of Heaven and our prayers through every possible means to draw them back into the fold.

And He *will* give us a song in our darkest night. Yes, He is faithful.

Transitions in Ministry

"If my husband decides to leave this church some-day," he'll have to go without me. I love this place and these people. It's my home."

The beautiful, blonde, and enormously talented pastor's wife in Tennessee was joking only a little. She has established a special bond with the people and has truly "nested" in that church family. It would be heart-wrenching for her to have to pack up and leave.

Heraclitus, a Greek philosopher, acknowledged the reality of transitions. He said, "Nothing endures but change." As sure as death and taxes, being uprooted from time to time happens in most lives—especially in the ministry. Facing change is a natural part of ministry life. By God's grace and enablement, we can move ahead into a new situation and find new levels of fulfillment in the Kingdom.

In his book *Married to a Pastor's Wife*, H. B. London Jr. poses the question "Does every assignment [in ministry] offer potential for satisfying ministry?" His response:

Yes, I believe it does. In our book *The Heart of a Great Pastor* we explain how every assignment can be holy ground. Journeying together in ministry has potential for pastors and their wives to discover beauty and meaning in every place. But they must intentionally recognize the possibilities, look at the opportunities, and count the joys. It takes close attention and testing our own stereotypes to make full use of moment-by-moment potential (H. B. London Jr., *Married to a Pastor's Wife* [Wheaton, Ill.: Victor Books, 1995], 272).

Still, there's the human factor. How do we move on without leaving our hearts behind? How do we protect and prepare our children for change? Is it possible to find satisfaction in every ministry assignment? How do we maximize transitions and find the balance we need for our families?

I really appreciate what Nancy Pannell wrote in her book *Being a Minister's Wife and Being Yourself*:

Responding to God's call to a new work is a step in faith. Every time we've stepped out in faith, God has shown us new dimensions of His power and provision. He hasn't always answered our prayers exactly as we anticipated, but He has always provided our needs. And in His graciousness, He has provided some of my wants that made the adjustments a little easier.

Recognizing it takes about a year to get oriented to new surroundings, I'd like to emphasize seven guidelines for making it through that trying first year.

- If you have children still living at home, give them top priority.

- Refrain from talking about your former church in the sense of making comparisons.
- Give yourself time to adjust before assuming new church responsibilities.
- Build bridges to the other staff wives.
- Allow yourself to develop at least one interest or hobby or friendship outside the church.
- Find a heart friend.
- Set some new goals, both immediate and long-term (Adapted from Nancy Pannell, *Being a Minister's Wife and Being Yourself* [Nashville: Broadman Press, 1993], 141-47).

—Nancy Pannell

Those of us who have transitioned within ministry have discovered anew the fulfillment of the promise of Phil. 4:13—"I can do all things through Christ who strengthens me" (NKJV)—even moving across the country or to the other side of the world.

There is also the transition that comes through maturity. In many aspects of ministry there is no mandatory retirement age, so it can be a bit challenging to determine when to step aside from pastoring or whatever our long-time ministry assignment may have been. When Gene turned 65, some questions began to surface about what our "plans" were. My prayer during the last couple of years of our pastoral ministry was that God would make it clear to my godly husband when it was His time for us to leave. And He did—miraculously. Gene says he gave himself a 66th birthday present on January 11, 1998. That was our last Sunday of pastoring after 27 years at that assignment.

Because God told Gene and me and made His timing very

clear, the doors He has swung open have been far beyond our imaginations. We have traveled the world—more than half a million miles. Our Father has fulfilled Hab. 1:5 in our lives during the subsequent years. We would not have believed it even if He had revealed those plans in advance. We are busier than ever, and Gene is preaching more than he did when he was pastoring. As a matter of fact, he often says, "If this is retirement, I think I'll get a job!" His definition of "retired" is that we've just put a new set of Michelins on our car.

I've always admired my cousin Patsy Pope. (People outside the family call her Pat.) She always knew she would marry a minister. Sure enough, she met Hugh Pope in college, and they have been married and in ministry together for more than 44 years.

Patsy has run the gamut of experiences as a minister's wife. From the first tiny little church to a number of other churches, all of which grew under their pastorate, to being Georgia district superintendent for their denomination, she and Hugh have enjoyed a life of service for the Lord. One of the highlights of their ministry years while Hugh was district superintendent was the blessing of helping plant several new churches. The pastor of one of those new churches was a young man who had been a part of the teen group in a church that Hugh and Patsy had pastored. He started Crossroads Community Church in Lawrenceville, Georgia, which now runs over 3,500 in attendance and is now Hugh and Patsy's home church.

As time approached for their retirement, they sat down one day and discussed the fact that they believed that God had something more for them. Although Hugh had suffered serious heart attacks and had undergone five bypasses, they knew that the Lord had spared them for special reasons.

In 1995 Hugh began traveling to Jamaica each year to conduct crusades. After he recovered from heart surgery in 2000, they felt led to start taking ministry teams there and incorporated Jamaica Faith Missions in 2001. Each year they take two teams to Jamaica to provide a crusade as well as to conduct a sewing school, computer school, medical clinics, children's ministries, pastors' seminars, and so on. They also send supplies for the poverty-stricken, teach Vacation Bible School, and lead a program called "Loaves and Fishes" to feed the hungry. The pastor uses the funds that are sent each month to help the ones he knows are most needy.

As a result of these crusades, Norwood Wesleyan Holiness Church in Jamaica has grown from 75 in 2000 to more than 300 now. How fitting that Hugh and Patsy's home church, Crossroads Community Church, helped to build a new sanctuary that seats 600—talk about passing the faith along!

Hugh and Patsy just sit back in amazement and give God all the glory for the great things He has done. In her words, "Never in our wildest dreams would we have imagined that God would have such a wonderful place of ministry for us in the years when most people are retiring. People ask us if we are retired, and we ask them, 'What does that mean?' As long as the Lord allows us, we want to serve Him and do all we can to see others come to know Him—who is life eternal."

This very day as I am working on this manuscript, Hugh and Patsy and a crew of volunteers are boarding an airplane in Georgia to fly to Jamaica to teach Vacation Bible School. I confess that I wish I could go on that trip to share the joy of ministering to the lost, hurting, and impoverished of Jamaica. I know that their rewards will be eternal!

I love what Kathryn Stephens Grant wrote in *Heart to Heart with Pastors' Wives* (p. 119) about "retirement" not being a word in God's vocabulary. She and her husband served as missionaries in Japan and then pastored a church in Washington, D.C. When they retired, both of them shifted into high gear. Her catalog of involvement in diverse ministries could be listed in several paragraphs. I really love her philosophy: "Knowing God's will is as significant for the mature seeker as it is for the young seeker." This is fully demonstrated in her life. It's true that God is never finished with us as long as we walk this planet. His plans are to bless our lives and fulfill us at all stages and ages.

So how do we make sure of God's will? How do we know when it's time to hang it up—to retire? Then how do we live through the transition with all its challenges? Once again, I turn to another mature ministry mate and dear friend—Marietta Coleman:

Clem and I sat at the breakfast table one morning talking about the often-discussed subject of when to retire. To our amazement, we discovered that we were both in agreement that now was the time. God had clarified this for both of us. So we announced our plans, and within the twinkling of an eye an offer came for Clem to be a "distinguished professor" at Gordon-Conwell Theological Seminary. This assignment meant that his gifts and special skills could be used to the fullest without many of the usual obligations of a professor. His extra time could be used in writing, speaking, and "walking through open doors" as the Lord led. I wasn't sure how I fit into that picture. But based on God's faithful provision over the years, I assumed He would provide a place for me. My only request was "I want to live with students—in the student apartment building." My friends thought that was so funny—and a little weird.

Living in the dorm was not the regular policy of the school, but they agreed to our request and prepared a four-room student apartment for us on the first floor of the dorm. The only mountains to climb before the move were going through the *last* graduation at Trinity Evangelical Divinity School without too many tears and deciding what to do with our house, which contained nearly 50 years of precious stuff. The second problem was soon resolved.

The Lord brought into our lives a precious student couple. Jennifer was at my house most Monday evenings with a student wives' group. I had been partially responsible for helping them to locate the apartment in which they were living. The most complimentary thing to say for the apartment was that it fit their budget. We proposed the idea that they move into our house when we left for our new assignment. We could live together anytime we returned for a visit. After thinking and praying about this unusual arrangement, all of us concurred that it was right.

A little surprise was lurking behind the scenes that only God knew about. I managed to get a nice spreading case of poison ivy. As I was complaining to the Lord about the itching and asking Him to help make it go away, I felt "it"—the lump every woman is told to check for each month. With the last commencement only days away, I decided to keep my secret. To put it mildly, those were emotion-filled days.

When the commencement tears were wiped away, it was time to attend to pressing issues. Clem was leaving for meetings in Europe, and we needed some answers before he left. They were not long in coming. One doctor appointment quickly moved me on to the next test or doctor. Very quickly I was scheduled for surgery. There were tears—and fears—but also supply. Years of experience had shown us that God does not waste our sorrows. He knows the way ahead. He supplies our needs.

First, there was the firm, tender, directive surgeon who assured my husband that he should go on to Europe and do his thing. In his absence all testing would be done, and when he returned we would be all set for surgery. Her firmness made this painful arrangement seem right. Second, another precious young couple had just helped me buy my first computer. (I was only 72 at the time!) That young student wife assisted me daily in learning how to use it. It was like a miracle that Clem and I could be in daily contact during that very stressful time. Third, as I began to share my situation with friends, one faculty wife whom I knew only casually came to me. She had just finished a very painful experience with cancer but offered to come alongside me as I went through my journey. What a blessing she turned out to be! During the summer I jokingly referred to my experience as "Cancer 101," hoping that I could learn enough that I wouldn't need to take Cancer 102.

Our summer schedule was drastically changed, but our young couple moved in with us anyway. Their arrival home each evening from work and school was a day brightener for Maggie and me. Maggie was their silly little dog who quickly became my cuddle and comfort buddy.

January came, and with energy at half-staff and my wig only slightly askew, we moved our possessions a thousand miles east. I began the attempt to make friends with students, figure how to fit into four small rooms, and determine to hang on to enough quarters for the washer and dryer. I was also trying to discern what my new ministry role would be.

One day I was taking some groceries over to an apartment that was being prepared for some new international students. A sweet young student wife insisted on driving me over. On the way home she hesitantly asked, "What would you say if someone told you they had cancer?" I immediately started a long detailed answer, then stopped and asked, "Do you know someone who has cancer?" She answered, "Yes. I do." There it was—one of those heart-tickling moments. It was time to share what I had learned in Cancer 101. God had not wasted my sorrows but had trained me for use. The next year another sweet young student wife and mother of two little children got that same frightening diagnosis. Once again I was privileged to come alongside her.

It seems that I am still enrolled in my cancer course, and the possibility of Cancer 102 is threatening. But what I have learned during the transitions of my life and ministry is that God is ever faithful. He stays close beside me. He always gives me an opportunity to use what comes across my pathway—both my sorrows and my joys. So I'll just wait with joy and anticipation to see what's around the next bend in my life or who will be moving in across the hall.

—Marietta Coleman

So as you can see, our dear friends have not retired. As we were finalizing this chapter, Clem and Marietta were preparing to go to Hong Kong to speak for a conference. The truth is, they've just strapped their suitcases tighter as they continue heading across the country and around the world.

Another dear friend of mine who is a ministry wife is Barbara Stephenson. The first day I met Barbara at the bank where we worked many years ago, I knew there was something very special about her. As we began to talk and share, it wasn't long before we became very good friends. When I invited her to visit our church, she readily accepted. That very first Sunday she stepped out into the aisle during the invitation and went forward to accept Jesus as her Lord and Savior.

Her husband, Reese, was another story—a hard case. Barbara was so excited about her new life with Jesus, and she wanted more than anything to share that with her husband. But he wanted no part of going to church. He had been brought up attending church, and the truth was, he knew that God wanted him to preach. But Reese had no desire to leave the six-figure income he enjoyed as an executive with the railroad. He knew he would have to sacrifice the "good life" he was living.

Finally, Barbara, Pastor and Mrs. Ted Holstein, and my family conspired to have the Stephensons for dinner at our house. The Holy Spirit was in charge from the very first moment. It was a divinely orchestrated evening. After dinner and getting my girls settled into bed, Pastor Ted presented the gospel to Reese. And that big old boy was finally ready to say yes. It was a glorious moment. That was more than 20 years ago.

Reese and Barbara became my dearest friends. To this day, I call her "Sister." They agreed to be godparents to my two daughters, Tami and Beth. Barbara began to teach in the Christian school that my daughters attended.

Sure enough, it wasn't long before God's call was confirmed. Reese and Barbara accepted the pastorate of a little country church, and he continued to work for the railroad.

A few months later, God's burning call could no longer be denied, and Reese resigned from the railroad to accept a call to a church in west Texas to pastor full time. His salary went from six figures annually to $150 per week. But God had a plan.

There were wonderful times. God opened the door for them to adopt two children, Scott and Leslie. The church grew, and God blessed. Through the years they transitioned several times, and there were tough situations as well—building programs, exhausting schedules—but the church grew. God kept blessing them. Their daughter, Jessica, was born. Life was good—but full of constant challenges.

As I was finishing this book, I felt compelled to touch base with Barbara. No book for ministry wives could be complete without a few words about my precious sister. As we talked, I asked her if she would have been excited about going into ministry if she had known 20 years ago all that she knows now. After all, they had given up a beautiful new home they had just built near the lake and a huge income to follow God's call on their lives. I knew that their retirement plan as pastors did not begin to compare with what the railroad would have offered after all of those years.

Without hesitating, Barbara exclaimed, "Oh, yes! Everything that has happened was all in the plan. You see, when God called Reese, He also called me. Sure, there have been problems with numerous transitions, people, finances, all kinds of things, so at times the journey has not always been joyful. But I must say that this life of ministry has been a trip I would gladly take once again."

I must confess that both of us were weeping over the phone. It was such a blessing to hear my dear sister delighting in serving the Lord. And I was reminded that our Father's benefits and blessings cannot be measured by earthly standards. After all, His retirement plan is divine. As a matter of fact, it is out of this world! Some day in heaven I know that there will be a huge throng of people lined up to say to Reese and Barbara, "Thank you for pointing me to Jesus."

Then Barbara really surprised me when she (as a fellow non-piano player) said, "Guess what! I'm learning to play the guitar." I just about fell over. I can't imagine her as a guitar-picker. But how like my dear sister Barbara to take the challenges of life, turn them over to the Lord, and pick up an instrument through which she can make a joyful sound, praising our Savior all the day long.

Till Death Do Us Part

I'll never forget the faces of our pastor and wife, Francis and Elsie Kether, the day they came by our home to say that she had been diagnosed with advanced breast cancer. My heart almost stopped as I was hit by the reality that, without a miracle from God, Elsie had only months to live.

Those weeks were anguished as the reports became more and more grave. Some days there seemed to be some hope, and then there would be another downward spiral. Pastor Fran desperately clung to any ray of hope, calling research centers across the country. We were deeply touched by his love, tenderness, and faithfulness during those excruciating times.

Finally the Sunday came when we knew it was just a matter of a few more hours. As the choir sang "Holy Ground," I could almost hear the hovering wings of angels fluttering. Some of us left the service and went to the hospital, where we told our dear friend and pastor's wife goodbye. Just a few hours later, the angels carried Elsie away.

Illness and death in a ministry home are very difficult. Not only is there the challenge of dealing with a chronic situation and all that's involved, but there's also the need to continue to minister and be there for those who are in our care. Without the enabling grace of the Lord, there's no way to get through such times. But because the promises are real and we truly can do all things through Christ, who gives us strength, (Phil. 4:13), we can survive the worst of times.

Joyce Mehl is a great model of His grace during illness and death. She and her husband, Ron, pastored a large church for many years while he lived with active leukemia and she managed her diabetes. She also writes about her life after Ron's death:

Till death do us part. . . . I rehearsed the words in my mind as I drove the freeway home. It was 11:30 P.M. I had just left the hospital where I had spent the last 17 days and nights by my husband's bedside in ICU. Ron had gone to be with the Lord earlier that night after a 22-year battle with leukemia.

We had shared our lives for 37 years, and now he was gone. Even in that brief time, driving home in the dark, I sensed I was beginning a new journey with the Lord. And I must admit, it was not a journey I looked forward to with much joy.

I remember reading about a woman who had to take a similar journey. I wonder if she felt anything like the way I felt that night, alone on that freeway. I wonder if she asked the Lord over and over, *Why is this happening?*

A Journey of Sorrow

Do you remember the story of Ruth and Naomi in the Bible? Naomi lived in the land of Israel with her husband, Elimelech, and their two sons. Caring for the duties of her small household, she probably lived as comfortably as other women of that time.

Then came the famine. I can imagine Elimelech coming home one day and announcing, "Naomi, call the boys. Pack up your things. We're moving to Moab."

Moab? When had children of Israel ever moved to that desolate, idolatrous nation? But these were desperate times, and Elimelech was out of options. He was doing what he could for his little family.

He probably promised Naomi that it would only be for a short time—until God answered the prayers of His people and ended the famine. She had no idea when she left on that journey what awaited her. She may have left some of her most prized possessions in Bethlehem, thinking she would soon return. Scripture, however, says she lived in Moab 10 years. And when the famine was over, she left behind something even more valuable than her possessions: her family. Her husband and two sons had died in the land of Moab.

Naomi planned on taking the journey back to Bethlehem alone. But she hadn't reckoned on Ruth. Her Moabitess daughter-in-law pleaded to go with her.

You probably know the rest of the story. God used Ruth to provide and care for Naomi. Ruth married Boaz, and the couple became great-grandparents of King David.

Did God know how hard it had been for Naomi to leave her home and friends to begin with? Hadn't it been enough for her to lose her husband in that strange land? Why her sons, too?

Was God with Naomi on this journey of desolation?

Yes, He was—every step of it, just as He is with you and me on every step of our journeys. Why? Because He has an eternal purpose. Just as He wanted to include Ruth and Naomi in His eternal plan to bring a Savior to a lost and sinful world, He also has an eternal purpose for you and me. That purpose may seem cloudy or shadowed right now. It may be wreathed with disappointment, sorrow, or loss. But if we belong to Him, we have a part to play in His eternal plans.

As the Lord told Israel, "I know the plans that I have for you . . . plans for welfare and not for calamity to give you a future and a hope" (Jer. 29:11, NASB).

God had plans—wonderful plans—for Naomi. But as she packed her few belongings to head back to Bethlehem, her eyes were darkened by grief. It must have taken a great deal of courage for Naomi to return to her hometown. After 10 long years, what awaited her there? And after all she had been through in Moab— well, who could blame her if she was apprehensive?

But the same loving Father who was with Naomi is with me. He allows nothing to touch me without first passing through the protection of His loving hands.

Something to Cling To

The apostle Peter reminds us that Satan walks about as a roaring lion, seeking whom he may devour. He feeds on our cares and gains strength on our anxieties. But as long as I am feeding on God's Word and trusting in His strength, anxiety and fear will find no place to reside in my life.

One of the most frequently repeated phrases in the Bible is "Do not be afraid." When my little grandchildren are afraid, they want to take hold of my hand. Courage comes when we have something to cling to.

When Jesus came walking across the sea, through the night and the storm, Peter called to Him from the boat, "Lord, if it's really You, tell me to come to You walking on the water." Jesus invited him to come, but no sooner did he step out of the boat than he began to look around at the sea and the storm. (Who wouldn't?) And, of course, he began to sink. What did Jesus do? He instantly reached out His hand and grabbed Peter.

He gave him something to hold on to. He didn't let him go under.

In the same way, when I cry out to Jesus in the dark and stormy times of life, when I reach for His hand, He holds me in His grip and pulls me closer to His side. The closer I get to Him, the more I trust His promises and hold on to His Word.

Daily Victories

The old hymn "Victory in Jesus" (written in 1939 by E. Bartlett) mentions that one day we'll sing the song of victory in heaven. I love those words! They remind me of the eternal victory that awaits us in heaven. In 1 Cor. 15 Paul tells us that death has been swallowed up in victory. For whom were these words written? Those who have already departed to be with the Lord?

No, I believe the victory is also for the one left behind. I have never, never—not in my whole life—been on a more difficult journey than the one I'm on now. But I'm so thankful for the daily victories that come from His hand. The One who has secured the ultimate victory for me has also provided little victories along the way—just to keep me encouraged and looking up. As part of that good plan of His, He brings me little touches of hope and comfort on those days when the journey seems too hard and too long, and the end seems too far away.

I sensed His touch in the words of my little granddaughter a few days ago. As I buckled her into her car seat after a day at preschool, she said, "Grandmommie, we had a wish day at school today."

"Oh, you did?" I said. "And what did you wish? Can you tell me?"

In that sweet and tender voice she said, "I wished I could live with you forever, because you don't have a husband anymore."

Immediately, the Holy Spirit reminded me of the words in Isa. 54:5—"Your Maker is your husband—the LORD Almighty is his name."

During the last year of Ron's life, his doctor wanted him to have as little physical contact with people as possible to avoid the infections he had no immune system to fight. This was hard on my husband, who had been a shepherd for nearly 30 years and so dearly loved his flock.

Ron had a small office at the church behind the platform. He went there before every service to wait until it was time for him to preach. There was a little window in the office that looked out onto the parking lot. He would stand at that window and peek through the blind before every service. No one could see him, but he could watch the people coming to church. He would call out the names to me as he saw the different individuals and families arrive. "Oh, here comes John. And there comes the whole Smith family. Those kids are the greatest! Here comes dear Mrs. Brown. I just love her. I hope she's feeling better these days." He named each one he knew and rejoiced over every one. I can still see and hear him. I can still feel his joy.

I often wonder if Jesus stands at the window of heaven and calls out to the Father with joy and anticipation the names of each one of us as we arrive. Perhaps He even asks, "How much longer, Father, before they all come home? Is it today?"

And we say, *Even so, come, Lord Jesus. You are our courage and victory until we enter that place where there is no more death and no more parting, and our journey will be complete. Until then, no path is too long, no night is too dark if You hold our hand.*

—Joyce Mehl

In Deletta Tompkins' case, it was she—the ministry wife—who suffered physically. Deletta Tompkins shares the story of her debilitating illness at the beginning of her marriage and ministry.

College graduation time had arrived. The event planning committee asked me to sing a solo at the baccalaureate service and play the organ for the commencement recessional. I accepted the request with gratitude and began to prepare for the big events.

My voice professor asked me to a sing a song from my senior voice recital, "O Rest in the Lord," from the oratorio *Elijah*, by Mendelssohn.

As I sang the song, little did I know that for years I would cling to the scripture promises in the song "wait . . . patiently . . . commit."

I had never planned to major in music. I didn't think I was qualified. In the spring of my freshman year, after praying and fasting one meal a day for two weeks, God used three different professors to speak to me, each suggesting that I major in music. God revealed His plan to me through godly professors. Miraculously, through the hard work of my parents and me, and through scholarships and God's strength, my school bill was paid before I received my musical education degree three years later *cum laude.*

She Can't Even Play the Piano!

Two weeks after graduation, I became very ill. I felt lifeless. Experiencing abdominal pain after work each day, I would go home to sleep as long as I could. I gained weight rapidly. My Christian physician diagnosed my problem and prescribed an injection of medication. Within two days I was much worse, so I was given another injection of the same medication.

Within hours I lost the ability to talk. In fact, I couldn't make a sound. I had experienced laryngitis before, but this time I knew things were different. I could not force a whisper, not a sound at all.

My condition worsened daily. My family physician referred me to a specialist who quickly diagnosed the original problem and prescribed an oral medication that would take several months to correct it. My secondary problem was a severe reaction to the injections that had caused my vocal cords to become so large that they couldn't vibrate. I could not make a sound.

Six weeks later, I made my first sound. But my voice sounded like a man's. When I walked into church, my voice professor cried. I could no longer sing solos or even participate in the church choir.

Later that summer I was offered a teaching position. I remember asking, "How can I teach music when I can barely talk?" My college professor said to me, "You can play the piano; you know how to teach music. You're regaining your speaking voice, so take the job."

I became the vocal music teacher of grades four through twelve. I loved teaching. Every day during senior high vocal music classes and vocal warm-up exercises, I tried to sing but couldn't. My only musical outlet was playing the piano and organ.

Finally one day I got a tiny little singing-voice sound. Excitedly, I telephoned my professor. He instructed me to keep vocalizing daily, carefully, and patiently.

After ten more months, I regained the full range of my voice but with very weak volume. Before the illness and injections, my voice was full and strong. After one year passed, my college professor insisted I go to a throat specialist, whose examination proved that my vocal cords were healthy with no scarring. Praise the Lord! He recommended a vocal therapist, but when we found out that the cost would be $50 per therapy session, we knew we could not follow that advice. Fifty dollars was a whole week's salary at the home missions pastorate my husband and I had taken.

Once again, my college vocal professor encouraged me. "You know how to sing correctly, and you know how to teach vocal development—now teach yourself to sing again!" He encouraged me to sing for him every time I returned to campus for a visit.

I exercised my voice daily. It went through every stage that a young man's voice does when it changes— plus the modulations that take place in a young lady's voice as she goes through puberty. Even my speaking voice had become uncontrollable.

One year passed into two. Spiritually I was numb. I felt nothing and experienced no emotion. I knew that my faith was a fact, but when I prayed, the heavens seemed so far away. Where was God? My life had been dedicated to using my talents for the Lord. Why didn't He answer my cries? Some of my family members suggested I file a malpractice lawsuit against the physician who prescribed the injections that caused the severe reaction. They commented, "After all, you've spent four years of hard work developing your voice, learning a career, and paying your bills."

My husband and I sought God's direction. We did not want to begin our ministry with a lawsuit. We must trust in God to provide!

Throughout this time God kept reminding me that He would heal me. Three years passed, then four, then five. We moved to pastor a church in a small town. The acoustics in that small sanctuary provided a rewarding sound, since there was no sound system there. The church members encouraged me to sing with my husband whenever I could. They didn't mind if my voice cracked or if I did not have the control I desired. They just wanted me to sing! It was during that time that I learned that I must lift my voice in praise to God whether or not it sounded the way I wanted it to.

Nearly seven years from the time I lost my voice, God restored my vocal praise to full voice again. It's interesting that once my voice became strong again, God called my husband into full-time evangelism. Our two children and I traveled weekends and summers to revivals, singing and supporting my husband's ministry. During those years we recorded two albums. I was singing in revival services five to six days a week, often without amplification.

Since God restored my voice, I have served for 28 years as a music pastor, almost six of those years as a song evangelist. Statistics show that most women my age cannot sing with the strength I've enjoyed. Sometimes I think maybe God has added the seven lost years back to this time in my life.

I've learned to rest and to wait patiently. God has fulfilled my heart's desires. He heard the melody of praise that arose from my heart even when I could not vocalize it. He truly does want us to commit all our ways to Him and trust in Him.

This is my story, and this is my song. God restored my voice. I continue to gratefully praise my Savior all the day long.

—Deletta Tompkins

Maintaining Confidences and Friendships

"I felt that I was going to explode if I didn't talk to somebody about what my husband said to me in front of a group of our church members. It hurt me so badly. But who can I tell? I certainly can't talk to the church people, and the last thing I want to do is to worry my family. I want to be able to forgive him and move on, but right now I'm too mad and hurt to even discuss it with him. Thanks for listening."

Through Shepherds' Fold Ministries, the ministry to pastors and their families that Gene and I founded in 1998, we have been blessed to become confidants to many ministry couples. We've become sounding boards for them as countless hurting shepherds and spouses have flocked to our door, called us, or communicated their concerns and heartaches via E-mail. We've eaten many meals across the table from anguished ministry leaders. Couples pastoring churches of a very few members to congregations in the thousands have sat in our living room weeping and pouring out their hearts. We count it a great privilege to be their "listening ears" and encouragers.

She Can't Even Play the Piano!

Unfortunately, not every ministry couple has found some-one safe in whom they can confide their deepest concerns. I remember talking with the pastor's wife of a very large church in another state who told me how happy she was to have found a confidant on the other side of the country. She said that having that outlet has added a new dimension to her life and ministry.

Another question ministry wives face is *Do we really need to know about everything that's going on in a church?* From talking with a number of wives, I would say the answer is no. Many of these women have shared with me that their hus-bands tell them after the fact about incidents and conflicts from which they have protected them. Conversely, I remember times when Gene received unfavorable notes that he never saw—because I threw them away. Ignorance can be bliss in some circumstances.

Joyce Rogers is a veteran ministry wife with vast experi-ence and insight. She shares about the issue of confidentiality in the ministry:

"You shouldn't have best friends in the church."

"The last pastor had a clique, and that caused a lot of trouble."

These words took root in my soul, and for the next 17 years in the ministry I didn't have a best friend. Up until then I had always had a best friend or best friends. In junior and senior high school my best friends were Betty, Bertha, and Betty Lou. During my first year in college, Chrissy became my roommate and ultimately a precious friend.

Adrian and I got married our second year in college. We met Millie and Bob, and Millie became my best friend. She had a baby before I did, and when I was expecting, she taught me many things about becoming a mother.

After college, Bob and Adrian went to the same seminary, so we still saw each other from time to time. One night Adrian was preaching in a nearby town. When he came home that night I could tell that something was seriously wrong. He had just heard that Millie had bulbar polio. We talked about it a long time before we went to sleep.

The next morning I was awakened by a phone call from Bob telling us that Millie had died. It was practically impossible to believe—my best friend had died. She was so young with two little girls, $1\frac{1}{2}$ and 3 years old. I remember vividly my deep grief in losing my friend.

In college we became friends with another couple, Joe and Joyce. The next year they joined us at seminary. Then we met Peter and Johnnie, and we all became good friends. After seminary we lived within 20 miles of each other; however, life was busy, and we didn't get to see each other very often. Then we moved to Tennessee, and I realized how much I loved these friends. We still see each other from time to time and will always be lifetime friends, but I miss the fellowship we had on a regular basis.

When we left seminary and moved to a new church, I heard someone say, "The last pastor had a clique, and that caused a lot of trouble." Inwardly, I declared, *I'll never cause trouble doing that.*

So for the next 17 years I didn't have any best friends in my church. I had many friends with whom I ministered, but I never shared my deepest feelings with anyone. As I look back now, I realize that a number of ladies made efforts to be my friends, but I allowed them only limited access to my feelings.

I was in a very busy period of life and raising four active children. I was involved with church activities, and Adrian was away from home a lot. He encouraged me to get a close friend, but I didn't really know how to go about doing that.

I remember feeling frustrated, but at the time I didn't realize that part of that feeling was the need for some good friends. God used a book by Oswald Chambers to speak to my heart and give me insight into my problem. I was expecting my husband to be my husband, lover, and best friend—my only friend.

Oswald Chambers wrote, "The human heart must have satisfaction, but there is only one being who can satisfy the last aching abyss of the human heart, and that is our Lord Jesus Christ" (Oswald Chambers, *The Place of Help*, 60). God spoke to my heart that day, saying, *You're trying to make Adrian play God in your life. He cannot meet every need you have for fellowship.*

It was still hard for me to make intimate friends. When we moved to another church, I determined that in this new situation I would make good friends. God did indeed send some wonderful friends into my life. Dot, Virginia, and I became very close. At first, Virginia and I met for lunch; I shared my vision for women's ministry, and we dreamed together. Then she opened her heart and shared some of her deep heartaches with me. I gradually began to share my heart with her.

Dot has always been a great encourager, and I love her as if she were my own flesh and blood. Virginia and Dot were 10 years older than I, but that never made a difference.

When Virginia was stricken with cancer, I couldn't

stand to see her suffer so much. With many tears and a broken heart, I asked God to take her home. When she died, I grieved the loss of another dear friend. Eventually Dot moved away, but we stay in touch and talk on the phone often. I call her my "forever friend."

Then God sent Juanita into my life. Juanita was a wonderful musician, and she had a servant's spirit. At first she was assigned to be my piano accompanist when I was asked to sing at a Valentine party. When I started teaching the children's new members class, I asked her to be my helper. For 30 years she played the piano and helped in any way she could. She became one of my dearest friends. She loved my children, and I loved hers. We loved music, and we both loved the Holy Land and traveled there together. We enjoyed traveling with our group to His land. She had the gift of hospitality and planned many lovely birthday parties in my honor and also for others.

She read the book *Sheltering Tree* and nicknamed herself my sheltering tree, and indeed, she was such a refreshment to me. Juanita was a survivor, and when diagnosed with breast cancer, she gallantly fought it for 10 years. As the end of her battle grew closer, Juanita came to the children's class with portable oxygen to play the piano and write on the board for me. It was in those days that I became her sheltering tree.

When Juanita went to be with the Lord, I planted a tree in our church courtyard with a simple brass marker at the foot that says "Sheltering Tree." Until now, only a few people knew this story—my family, her family, and a few others. Before she died. I told her what I planned to do in her honor, and she was so pleased.

It's still difficult for me to initiate friendships, but God has been so good to send special friends to me.

Such is my sweet friend, JoAnn, whom I met on a trip to the Holy Land. She became friends with both of my daughters and also with me. She has blessed my life most of all with her unconditional love and also with her wonderful gift of decorating. Her special touch permeates my home.

Marli is the latest friend God has sent into my life. I originally met her on the pages of a magazine article. She wrote about how we as women could pray for "women behind the veil" and help reach out through a radio program called "Women of Hope" to needy women around the world. Through this contact I have personally met Marli. I see her only occasionally, but God has knit my soul to hers through the bond of prayer.

There are other friends with whom I have dared to open my heart over the years. They have been wonderful blessings to me, and I trust that I have been a blessing to them.

I was recently invited to join a group of ladies for a monthly luncheon. These ladies are very active in ministry, but the purpose of the group is merely to cheer each other on. They've been a genuine delight to me. Years ago I would have thought I didn't have time for a group like this, but now I realize that I need these friendships.

Finally, one of God's greatest gifts to me is my husband's administrative assistant of 31 years. Linda is a precious friend and my greatest prayer partner.

I believe God means for us to have special friends with whom we can share our joys and sorrows and to help us bear our heavy loads. Even Jesus had His special friends—His disciples, His inner circle: Peter, James and John; and close friends He greatly loved, such as Mary, Martha, and Lazarus.

I encourage you to have friends who are intimates. Ask God to send you the right kind of friends. However, always have a smile, and be friendly to everyone. Don't always rush to your best friends when you're at church; avoid leaving others out.

I not only want to have special best friends, but I also want to be a good friend. The scripture says, "There is a friend who sticks closer than a brother." (Prov. 18:24) And indeed, "Better is a friend who is near than a brother who is far off." (Prov. 27:10, JB)

—Joyce Rogers

Kathy Slamp has many years of experience as a ministry wife, and she is in great demand as a speaker and writer. Kathy shares about the need for confidentiality in the ministry.

The parsonage is unlike any other home I know of. My father and my brothers were pastors, and my husband is still a pastor. What a diverse lot we pastors and wives are! Despite our varied and abounding differences and giftedness, those of us who are fortunate enough to live in the parsonage have a lot in common. We're exposed to some of the darkest sides of humanity, and yet we're blessed to know and partner with some of God's choicest saints—those wonderful people known as parishioners.

There's one thing in particular we have in common that's a lesson we must learn early on if we want to survive in the parsonage—to keep our own counsel. For the quiet, timid ones, this is a bit simpler than for those of us who are more outgoing. But regardless of our temperaments, learning to zip our lips or bite our tongues (or whatever we choose to call it) is a parsonage survival must. Once again, I know—from personal experience.

Most people really do mean well. Occasionally, however, there are those who have different agendas, and if we aren't cautious, it's easy to become ensnared in someone's evil trap. Our church members and friends will never have the same perspective as we do. Just when we think we've made a close friend, he or she will either disappoint us, or we'll disappoint him or her. A few funny incidents have occurred over the years that illustrate this: Once while buying groceries, I came around the corner of the aisle pushing a basket of food and supplies and came face to face with a lovely woman from our church. At first she was speechless but then choked out a hilarious greeting, "Oh," she said somewhat aghast, "I just never thought about it. I guess you have to buy groceries just like the rest of us."

Whether we like it or not, whether it's fair or not, and whether we would love to change it or not, the fact remains that some of our church people may tend to put us on a proverbial pedestal. I came really close that day to saying, "No, we don't buy groceries like the rest of you. God provides manna from heaven. I'm just here buying condiments to go with it."

While this incident is humorous, there were other times that weren't so funny. It's fairly easy for us to say or do something that can ultimately be harmful to the church, our husband's ministry, or hurt us personally. It's never intentional; it just happens in a moment of human weakness.

There remains an isolation and loneliness that

comes from being set apart—there are no two ways about it. In our case, these feelings have brought my husband and me together in a unique bond that is only enhanced by the separation created by his calling. It's not a curse; it's just the way things are. At this point in the journey, I couldn't think of a life I would like better. Keeping that lip zipped doesn't rob me of my individuality, and it doesn't inhibit my lifestyle. But it's a vital lesson we learn early on that protects us and keeps us above the fray. In 2 Cor. 13:4-5 we read, "We also are weak in him, but we shall live with him by the power of God. . . . Examine yourselves, whether ye be in the faith; prove your own selves" (KJV). When it's all said and done, we're responsible for what we say. God can help us, regardless of age or temperament, to be a treasure and not a hindrance to the body.

—Kathy Slamp

Frances Simpson, a veteran ministry wife, has further insights into confidentiality.

"Please don't tell anyone!" How often have you heard that?

Sometimes it's a flippant request, but sometimes it's an anguished plea. If we're good listeners, we'll accumulate a lot of information through the years—good and bad—and what we do with it is our moral responsibility.

I remember the admonition given to us when our husbands were seminary students: "Treat everyone the same. Don't foster special friendships within your congregation." At the time I questioned that warning. In retrospect, I have found it to be wise counsel.

Recently, a young pastor's wife asked me, "Who is a safe person with whom I can share?" My answer has been the same for nearly half a century: "Occasionally you might find another ministry wife in whom you can confide. Just remember: once you've spoken, those words may possibly be repeated—and not necessarily exactly as you spoke them. So be careful."

Many times when people share confidences with me, I ask, "May I discuss this with my husband?" Almost without exception they'll say, "Yes, you may." However, my husband usually has enough weight to carry, so I try to be careful not to load him down with unnecessary baggage. I have found that God is a steady, available, and ever-ready listener—a counselor, friend, and one who can give us discernment in the stickiest situations.

Paul lays out the perfect formula for maintaining friendships in Col. 4:6: "Let our conversation be always full of grace, seasoned with salt, so that you may know how to answer everyone."

Problems arise in every ministry, and we have to make decisions. Do we want to defend our families, or is our main focus that of building God's kingdom? Will what we say build up the Church or tear it down? Will it bring glory to God or to Satan?

In one of our churches we discovered that two of our most respected and loved leaders were engaged in an illicit sexual relationship. Both of the participants had many family members in the church. Their affair made it necessary to remove both of them from all of their church responsibilities. I still remember the night I stood before the choir and announced that I would be leading them for the next few weeks. Scared? Yes. Less qualified than the previous leader? Definitely. But even though I was not able to offer any explanation, I began what turned out to be a three-year assignment. A public statement was never made. Instead, my husband called for special prayer and fasting. And the two individuals were later reconciled to God. Gossip and offensive talk could have destroyed much of that congregation and ruined the reputations of those responsible.

On another occasion in a different church we were pastoring, unexpected visitors showed up at our door late one evening. A leading couple had come to accuse us of opposing the wife's appointment to a board position. We were taken totally off guard and tried to appease them and assure her of our confidence and faith in her abilities. The next day we sent them a beautiful bouquet with a note expressing our love and appreciation. For several weeks she nursed her wounded pride and talked freely about her sense of rejection. At that time I remember thinking that if I decided to tell the truth and set the record straight, it could split that large church right down the middle. When we eventually left for a new assignment, it was rewarding to have her throw her arms around me and say, "You have been the perfect pastor's wife." I knew better, but I thanked God for helping me to keep my mouth shut and my heart open to His leadership.

I remember another lady who called us often to talk about the shortcomings of a "friend" of hers. Finally, one day when she called, I believe it was the Lord who inspired me to say, "Evidently our friend is having a hard time right now. Let's pray for her." I began to pray for both of them. She never called to complain about the other lady again.

A great reminder is found in Eccles. 3:7 that reminds us that there is "a time to be silent and a time to speak." Often it becomes a matter of the heart rather than the tongue. When we fall short, be quick to apologize and redeem the situation.

When it comes time to leave a church, it's extremely important that we don't attempt to settle any old scores. That's especially true if there has been conflict or we've been mistreated. Do we want to vindicate ourselves, or do we want to preserve the unity of the church? Remember: God has admonished us to leave avenging to Him. Our responsibility is to build up the church for the next pastoral family. We must be careful not to allow Satan to trick us into defending ourselves at the expense of God's kingdom.

Friends—we want them and need them. A healthy church—that's our ministry assignment. And one of the best ways to preserve both areas is to "zip our lips."

—Frances Simpson

As I pointed out in the beginning of this book, the contributors may have varied opinions as to how we're to respond to different situations. The best plan to follow is to listen carefully to the still, small voice of our Creator. I love the words of Prov. 3:5-6—"Trust in the LORD with all your heart and lean not on your own understanding; in all your ways acknowledge him, and he will make your paths straight." In today's vernacular we might add, "and he will tell you when to zip or unzip your lips!"

My husband, as do many ministers, tries always to remember to check his pants zipper before going to the platform before each service. However, he had an episode or two of making the discovery that his pants were unzipped when he was already standing before the congregation. One of Gene's staff bought a huge poster of a fly and hung it on the back of the restroom in Gene's study. That made it the last thing he saw before he left the study for the sanctuary. And it really worked!

Maybe it would be a good idea for us to hang a mental fly over our lips to guard our words. Then we could assure that our "lip zipper" is closed at the proper moments.

Dealing with Temptation

The chemistry between Tanya, the senior pastor's wife, and the new youth minister, Brendon, was immediately apparent. From the first staff dinner they hit it off as though they had been friends for years. His outgoing personality and sense of humor had her in stitches in the first 30 minutes. It had been a long time since she and her husband, Stephen, had laughed that loud and long. He was always too busy with the demands of the church.

The next day Brendon called Tanya to bounce a couple of ideas off of her. She was flattered that he wanted her input. That weekend when she was shopping at an office supply store, Brendon came up behind her and said, "Look who's here!" They went next door for a quick burger and laughed as they ate lunch. Tanya felt young and giddy as they giggled together.

Almost before they realized what was happening, Tanya and Brendon were enmeshed in an emotional affair. They talked on the phone several times a day. Then there were the pats on the shoulder and the furtive hugs.

One day Brendon stopped by the house to pick up a book.

As he was leaving, he reached out and drew Tanya into an embrace. At that moment her four-year-old came into the room and asked, "Mommy—what are you doing?" It was a light-bulb moment for Tanya. She pulled away and said good-bye to Brendon. She spent the rest of that day thinking, *What was I doing?* She was blasted with the reality that she had been flirting with losing everything of value in her life. From that time on, her relationship with Brendon never went beyond appropriate boundaries.

All of us know where this fictitious scenario could have led. Unfortunately, similar circumstances have led to a multitude of disasters and the deaths of countless marriages and ministries. How can we protect ourselves?

Ever since Eve succumbed to the wiles of the serpent, we've had to deal with Adam's excuse, "She made me do it!" I'm positive that Eve did not wrestle Adam to the ground and force-feed the fruit to him. But it made him feel better to shift the blame to her shoulders.

The truth is that ministry wives are sometimes quite vulnerable. Being in ministry can be very lonely at times. If proper boundaries are not established and maintained, spouses can feel abandoned and second rate. It's essential that we guard against the temptation to become too friendly with sympathetic men at work or at church.

Ministry couples may not struggle with the distinctly black-and-white issues of right and wrong. After all, the top 10 were written in stone by God's own hand! But the gray areas tend to entrap us. Those of us who are in ministry are not immune from attacks from the enemy. We should always remember that "forewarned is forearmed."

Evangelists who travel the country have many opportunities to peer into the fishbowl of parsonage life. These ministry couples are often accepted as kind, warm, loving, short-term, intimate confidants. Linda Armstrong and her husband have become "safe people" to hundreds of pastors and their wives in the many years that they have journeyed across the highways of our land in their big bus. She shares some of the snares and pitfalls for ministry couples that she has observed.

I vividly remember the way my heart fluttered when my husband, Leon, said, "Honey, I think God wants us to resign as associate pastors, buy a bus, and travel as evangelists." Nearly a quarter of a century and hundreds of thousands of miles later, I can't believe some of the experiences we've had. Breakdowns, split-second timing, new faces each week, and all kinds of adventures have kept our lives from being boring.

One of things we've enjoyed most along the way is communicating with ministry couples. Leon and I have been privileged to become confidants to many of these leaders of flocks.

Hundreds of ministry wives have poured out their most intimate struggles and deepest needs to me. Their stories are varied. Many have shared about areas in which they've been tempted. And even though each wife feels her difficulty is unique, I've discovered that these wives all share many common factors. It's the recurring themes of these temptations that encourage me to tell each ministry wife that she's not alone.

God's Word offers great comfort. "Remember that the temptations that come into your life are no different from what others experience. And God is faithful. He will keep the temptation from becoming so strong that you can't stand up against it. When you are tempted, he will show you a way out so that you will not give in to it" (1 Cor. 10:13, NLT).

I believe that the best way to deal with these difficult issues is to divide life's perplexing situations into three categories—tests, trials, and temptations.

TESTS: As we face the tests of life and rely on God's Word for instructions, we're reminded that His power and grace are sufficient for each difficulty.

TRIALS: Trials are simply problems of life. Every human being faces distress, disappointment, discouragement, disease, and death. Although God has the power to relieve us from these difficulties, He doesn't bring them. They're simply part of the human condition.

TEMPTATIONS: Temptations are conditions the enemy uses in an attempt to destroy our relationships with God, family, and friends. God doesn't orchestrate them. We read in James 1:13, "When tempted, no one should say, 'God is tempting me.' For God cannot be tempted by evil, nor does he tempt anyone." Temptations sometimes come as a result of allowing our minds to wander from God. Again in James we read, "Each one is tempted when, by his own evil desire, he is dragged away and enticed" (1:14). Sin comes if we neglect to deal effectively with temptations. "Then, after desire has conceived, it gives birth to sin; and sin, when it is full-grown, gives birth to death" (1:15).

Although there's some overlap in these three areas, many temptations begin as trials as the enemy often uses trials to lead us into temptations. These trials fall into three general actions and reactions: giving in, giving out, and giving up. When such trials are not brought into check by the Holy Spirit and the Word of God, they lead to serious temptations that can divide the church and destroy families.

Giving In

Many ministers' wives feel they need to be all things to all people in the church. They feel that regardless of how hard they try, it's seldom good enough. The temptation is to feel guilty and inadequate. This can result in a more serious temptation—the feeling that they've failed.

There are times when a ministry wife has a duty and responsibility thrust upon her for which she doesn't feel adequate. It's not that she doesn't want to do it—she simply feels *unable* to accomplish it. But since the task must be done and no one else will help, she attempts to complete the assignment and falls short of the expectations. She begins to feel inadequate in every area of ministry and life. This is compounded if her husband is not around to help or is critical. Ultimately, a helpless feeling overwhelms her, and she begins to feel that she can't do anything right. Insecurities inundate her, and subsequent ministry attempts may become obligations to be completed rather than joyful opportunities to serve the Lord and His Church.

In our visits to churches across the country, I've heard common sentiments expressed by pastors' wives such as "I can't be myself. The people at my church have so many expectations of me, and I just can't be the person they want me to be. They expect too much." That situation causes them to feel torn between their giftedness versus expectations. The temptation to give up is born. Some wives withdraw into a shell because they start feeling that they can't please anyone—not even their husbands.

Giving Out

A minister's wife admitted to me once that her greatest temptation was simply to think too highly of herself. She had so many abilities and gifts that her temptation was to just go ahead and complete assignments because she could do them better than most of the other church members. The problem was that others in the church needed to feel useful and involved in ministry. Her temptation was to try to do too much.

Many gifted ministry wives who have the ability to organize and efficiently complete tasks can become so preoccupied that they neglect their personal devotions and quiet time with the Lord. It can be quite a balancing act since there are so many jobs to be done. It's essential to understand that it's not a sin to say no. One of the best things a ministry wife can do for herself and her ministry is to avoid the tendency to try to do it all. By encouraging others to become involved, laypersons can also enjoy the fulfillment that comes as a result of ministry.

Giving Up

I have encountered many wives who are ready to give up on their husbands, their churches, and occasionally even God. Sometimes this feeling has developed because the wife feels that her husband consistently puts church matters and church members first and that she rarely has his undivided attention. In most cases it's not that he doesn't love her—rather, it's because of the 24/7 expectations of ministry. Every profession is demanding. Talk to a doctor's wife. Mention your loneliness to an insurance agent's wife. Many feel neglected. But for some reason, we think ministry should be different. It isn't.

It's certainly true that some ministers tend to feel guilty when relaxing at home. As a result, his wife and family begin to feel neglected. That can lead to self-pity and a desire to give up on everything. I've talked with wives who have been tempted to turn to a sympathetic coworker or friend who is willing to take the time to listen. That's one of the enemy's most insidious tricks. Without realizing it, confidences may lead to entanglements that can grow into full-blown affairs. Those who succumb to that temptation end up destroying their families, ministries, and lives.

There's only one way to overcome these temptations. The formula seems too simple, but it still works: *communicate with each other and pray.*

I love to remind hurting ministry wives to really believe "I can do everything through him who gives me strength" (Phil. 4:13). By truly embracing that promise, we can stay on course and finish the task.

At this writing, I find myself praying for the pastor's wife with whom I've spent time this week. She has many needs and concerns. I hear the bus starting, and I turn to see her coming toward me. She says, "Can I have one more hug?" As I embrace her gently, I whisper, "You can do this. God will help you. Don't be discouraged. He's by your side. Remember Phil. 1:5-6—'Because of your partnership in the gospel from the first day until now, being confident of this, that he who began a good work in you will carry it through to completion until the day of Christ Jesus.'"

As Leon and I head down the highway, I'm comforted to know that the Lord is with us on the journey of life. He'll guide and guard us from all the snares of the enemy—if we let Him. My heart lifts as I reflect on how God has enabled me to bring comfort to another hurting ministry wife. And I begin to feel excitement for what's around the next turn.

—Linda Armstrong

As Linda mentioned, a far more subtle temptation for ministry wives is to try to be all things to all people. Since that's obviously impossible, it's imperative that ministry wives be themselves. A pastor's wife recently told me that in her younger days she tried to adapt to expectations of the church members by attempting to adjust her personality to suit various situations and challenges. She chuckled when she told me that she realized that was not a good idea when she found that she couldn't remember which personality she had been using at different times. So she tossed aside the multi-personalities and vowed to just be her best self. And the people in the church came to love her—the *real* her! Beverley London addressed this in my book *Unshakable Faith for Shaky Times*:

> If I had any advice to give to other pastor's wives, it would be in one simple phrase: Be yourself. And have faith in God's guidance. With the encouragement of your husband, do your best. Find a pace you can keep without exhausting yourself, and regardless of the size of your church, view it as your sanctuary—a place for your family to call home, a place to deepen the roots of your faith (131).

Again, there are multiple temptations, tests, and trials that come into the lives of those in ministry. Staying focused on our Lord will enable us to resist the tempter's snares. We can have victory over the obvious entrapments as well as those that are less evident. Staying real and being transparent can become a great challenge when we consider the many issues that we'll face in ministry. By God's grace we can be all *He* intends us to be.

For Better or for Worse

8

"You know, God didn't call me to preach. He called my husband. I'm sick and tired of never seeing him and of the constant pressures. I just don't need this. Besides, I have my own career in real estate. Of course, the best time for me to show houses is on weekends. So there are more and more Sundays when I just can't make it to church. I feel that there's no use in trying to make it work any longer. We have nothing in common. Our kids are grown, and I'm financially independent. He doesn't need me, and I don't really need him anymore. We'd both be better off without trying to keep up the façade of this marriage. The church people will adjust. We'll probably end up just going our separate ways."

As I heard these words from a pastor's wife of more than 30 years, I cringed. This was not the first time I had heard similar feelings voiced by a pastor's wife. Many long-time ministry marriages are falling apart today. What happened to commitment for life—for better or for worse?

I like to ruminate about Peter's wife, an Early Church ministry wife. One of my favorite Bible characters is Simon Peter. I relate so well to his failures, and I surely want to be more like the post-Pentecost rock upon which our Lord established His Church. But have you ever wondered what it was like to be Peter's wife—to live with him and travel with him? We read about her in several passages—although never by name. We know that her mother lived with her and Peter and had felt the healing touch of the Master. It's quite possible that Peter's wife was part of the entourage who traveled with Jesus and the disciples helping to care for their needs. She could have been present for many of the great events and miracles throughout Jesus' earthly ministry. I would like to peer behind the miniscule snapshots and see this woman who stood by her man through great challenges.

Wouldn't it be wonderful to know how Peter described the Transfiguration to her? Or what did he tell her about the day he walked on water—for a few steps at least? Peter was an impulsive man with a tendency to quit when things went against him. When he came home in a despairing mood of abject failure, he might have said the equivalent of these words: "Honey, I blew it again!" I wonder how she reasoned with him, cautioned him, and encouraged him to rise above the trials and his failures. How did she console Peter after he failed abysmally with his denials before the Crucifixion? I believe our Lord gave this precious ministry mate wisdom as she comforted, encouraged, and challenged him. I'm sure there were times when they disagreed. How did they handle conflict? Do you think it's likely that God gave her a calming nature to balance Peter's impetuous one? Regardless of these details that we can't know, there's no doubt about her commitment.

Speaking of commitment, we know that despite the hardships they encountered, she traveled with Peter. Paul records in 1 Cor. 9:5 that Peter took his "believing wife" along with him on some of his missionary journeys. There's no doubt that she was a noble woman and faithful partner who endured the rigors of primitive travel and accommodations as she faithfully followed Peter. Although their personalities may have been quite different, I believe the Lord balanced them so that they presented a godly pair who served together in spreading the gospel. And I'm sure they celebrated the resulting harvest.

Tradition tells us that Peter's wife was with him in those final hours in Rome. Accordingly, it is told that when the hour for their deaths came, the executioners chose to kill her first. As she was led out of their cell to die, Peter comforted her with the words "Remember the Lord!" Somehow I picture her walking tall and bravely to her death. When the time came for Peter to die, according to tradition, he begged to be hung head-downward because he felt unworthy to die in exactly the same way as his Lord had.

That was ultimate commitment to the Lord and to each other. Peter and his wife were partners together in life and in death, and they are eternally sharing heaven together. Oh, I really want to meet this precious woman of faith when I get to heaven. Think of the experiences she can share—as Paul Harvey says, "the rest of the story."

Billy and Ruth Bell Graham comprise one of the best-known ministry couples alive today. Both of them are in their mid-80s now and have more than half a century of experience in the spotlight of ministry. They've encountered just about every possible difficulty throughout these years of high visibility, ministry, and pressure. I've long admired Mrs. Graham's wisdom and wit. So now we turn to this godly woman for insight on how to victoriously survive as a ministry team.

Where two people agree on everything,
one of them is unnecessary.

A group of ladies from the "Tab," where Bill was student minister, gave me a bridal shower shortly before we were married. Each of them wrote a bit of advice on a piece of paper and gave it to me. The above quote was the pick of the lot.

How often that saying came to mind, and how necessary I felt!

I have met wives who did not dare to disagree with their husbands. I have met wives who were not permitted to disagree with their husbands. In each case, the husband suffered. Either he became insufferably conceited, made unwise judgments, tended to run roughshod over other people, or was just generally off-balance. However, it is a good thing to know how to disagree and when.

Here are a few suggestions out of my own experience: First, define the issue (and make sure it is worth disagreeing over); next, watch your tone of voice and be courteous (don't interrupt, and avoid rude, unkind, or unnecessarily personal remarks); third, stick to the subject; fourth, stick to the facts; and fifth, concede graciously.

As for when to have a disagreement, this takes both sensitivity and ingenuity on the part of the wife as well as the husband.

For one thing, it is not wise to disagree with a man when he is tired, hungry, worried, ill, preoccupied, or pressured. (That doesn't leave me many opportunities.)

Nor does it pay to argue with your husband unless you are looking your very best. The woman who argues with her hair in rollers has ten strikes against her to begin with.

And avoid arguing when you are boiling mad over some issue. Sleep on it first, if possible, then try to discuss it calmly and objectively. Likely as not, by then you won't be able to remember what you were upset about in the first place.

A Christian wife's responsibility balances delicately between knowing when to submit and when to outwit. Adapting to our husbands never implies the annihilation of our creativity, rather the blossoming of it.

—Ruth Bell Graham

From Ruth Bell Graham, *It's My Turn* (Old Tappan, N.J.: Fleming H. Revell Co., 1982), 54-55. Used by permission.

"We are such opposites! I know the old saying that opposites attract is supposed to be a good thing. But I just wish that we could somehow agree on one thing!"

As I listened to Suzette, a young pastor's wife, I remembered something I had read in my dear friend Jill Briscoe's book *Faith Enough to Finish* about learning to celebrate our differences.

I said, "Suzette, if you'll give me a couple of days, I want to get a copy of Jill's book for you so you can read about this concept of rejoicing because you're not alike." On my way home I stopped by our Christian bookstore and bought the book. I could hardly wait to get it to Suzette.

Celebrating the differences means being determined to appreciate the ways people are different. If you concentrate on one major difference at a time and work on making a real mental effort to find something you can appreciate about it, you will succeed. When you have found a major difference, think about it in a determinedly positive way. Next, pray about it, and thank God for your partner and the major difference you have found.

Because Stuart and I are so very different, we have

had the opportunity to do a lot of this sort of thing. When we first came to the States in 1970, people began to ask us to speak together. Often they would ask us to speak about marriage. I was so excited. Up to this point, we had both been busy speaking, but on different sides of the Atlantic. Now we could put our gifts together for the Lord.

I remember our first joint speaking engagement. It was in Chicago, and it was a marriage retreat. True to form, I began to prepare at least three months in advance. "What shall we speak about?" I asked my husband happily.

"Jill, it's three months away—we'll talk about it the week before," answered my husband.

I was horrified. I could never be properly prepared a week before an event. "Well, at least let's choose the passage of Scripture so I can be thinking about it," I suggested.

"Jill, I have a church to run," replied my husband. "We don't need to start on this yet. We have dozens of meetings before this one."

I tried not to bug him about it but did anyway—to no avail. The week before came, and I was panicked. "Do you know yet what we are doing?" I asked him in an accusing voice.

"Not yet, Jill," he replied unconcerned. "I have a funeral and a deacon's meeting to go to before I'll have time to pull it together." The day arrived, and we had only a vague idea of what we would do. "Don't worry about it," my husband kept saying. "You'll see, all sorts of things will come to mind just when you need them to!"

All sorts of things were coming to mind, but not the sorts of things that should have been! Getting into the car with a strained silence between us, I promptly burst into tears and wept copiously all the way to Chicago! "Whatever shall we do?" I sobbed as we arrived at the venue.

"Why don't we both get up there and analyze what went wrong?" suggested Stuart cheerfully. "Then we can talk it out in front of the people and explain how we resolve a conflict in our marriage!"

It was too late to do anything else. To my absolute amazement, I found myself up on the platform talking the whole thing over in front of a few hundred interested people!

Stuart began by explaining that we had had a difference of opinion on the way to the meeting and they were very welcome to listen in as we resolved it. And so we talked it out as we usually solved our disputes. We discussed how very opposite we are, how our way of doing things is so drastically different, and how it causes problems all the time. Then I apologized for my attitude, and Stuart apologized for his. Next, Stuart said what he appreciated about my way of diligent preparation, and I told him how I admired his wonderful ability to pull things together so quickly. We celebrated each other's differences verbally.

Then we forgot all about the three hundred interested onlookers and told each other how we would begin to make allowances for the other and show consideration for the way each of us worked. We thought up some compromises both of us could make and promised to make them. We smiled at each other, laughed a bit, gave each other a hug, and then suddenly we remembered we had an audience! So Stuart opened his Bible and did what he does best—teach. He spoke on Ephesians 5:21-33, the classic text about how husbands and wives should treat each other. I listened carefully and thought of illustrations from our marriage that I could use when he had finished. The day flew by. It was wonderful!

That incident happened at least twenty-five years ago, but just this month a man said to me, "Do you remember coming to Chicago to talk about marriage? You came on stage and looked as though you had been crying for a week!" He had been there! "I have never forgotten that," he said.

I bet he hadn't! Neither have I because that was the day Stuart and I began to work on "celebrating the differences" and using those differences as weapons—not against each other, but for God and his Kingdom.

—Jill Briscoe

From Jill Briscoe, *Faith Enough to Finish* (Wheaton, Ill.: Tyndale House Publishers, 2001), 121-23. Used by permission.

Let's hear again from Ruth Bell Graham.

Bill's and my tastes differ (in books, music, style, décor, food, hobbies, and so forth). Even our forms of relaxation differ. I go for a good book. He, immersed in books most of the time as it is, used to play golf, now runs two miles a day. Grateful for the excuse of an arthritic hip, I can walk but not run.

Our temperaments differ. By nature I am easygoing to the point of laziness and am basically optimistic. Bill is highly disciplined and drives himself unmercifully. The family affectionately refers to Bill as "Puddleglum"—a modern-day Jeremiah.

"Puddleglum," for those of you who have not been introduced to this delightful individual, appears in one of C.S. Lewis's children's stories, "The Silver Chair." He is the extraordinary character known as a Marshwiggle, who joins Eustave and Jill after they are sent by Aslan to find Prince Rilian. (If you are getting confused, go buy the book. It's worth it.)

Puddleglum has the boundless capacity for seeing the grim side of every situation. Each simple statement or dire prediction is either preceded or followed by, "I shouldn't wonder." In the end he turns out to be the most sterling character in the entire book, true-blue to the core.

The classic case of my Puddleglum's "I shouldn't wonder" attitude came once when we landed at the Miami airport. Bill had to stay, while I was to fly home. He checked the weather and learned it was not good in Atlanta, Georgia, where I would have to change planes for Asheville, North Carolina.

"You probably won't be able to land," he predicted. "If not, I don't know where you will go—probably on to New York City. But if they try to land, I hope you make it; Atlanta is one of the busiest airports in the United States. And if you do, I'd advise you to spend the night in a motel—if you can get a room, which I doubt—as a lot of planes will be grounded and the motels will be full. In that case, rent a car, if you can get one, and drive home. But drive carefully because . . ."

You guessed it ". . . you could have a wreck!"

Still laughing as I climbed aboard the plane, I pulled out my notebook to jot down this choice bit of "I shouldn't wonder" before I forgot it. Incidentally, the plane landed safely, I transferred with no trouble, and the plane to Asheville made it without difficulty. But this was The Classic, the statement we as a family have enjoyed to the fullest, the one which even Bill had a good laugh over when I read it back to him.

At the same time, let me say that there is no one—but no one—who is better in an emergency than Bill. He remains calm while his mind races like a jet airplane, and he is capable of making correct decisions quickly and decisively.

—Ruth Bell Graham

From *It's My Turn*, Ruth Bell Graham (Revell Publishers: 1982), 62-63. Used by permission.

There's no doubt that being in ministry brings great challenges to marriage. There are some cardinal rules that work regardless of what may come.

- Stay true to your commitment to God and your marriage vows.
- I know a pastor's wife who says they never discuss the D (divorce) word. Murder? Maybe!
- Find a safe confidant and/or counselor.
- Be 100-percent loyal to your spouse.
- Communicate.
- Never go to bed angry.
- Pray together each day—preferably in an embrace. Gene and I have shared this precious time ever since our wedding day.

Ministry couples can have great marriages and wonderful families. It's a matter of commitment and perseverance. Establish acceptable boundaries, and stay within them.

All the dear ladies in this book would encourage you to stay true to the promises in your wedding vows. By God's grace and enabling power (in my daddy's words), we can "keep on keeping on"—for better or for worse. We can celebrate our differences and trust the Lord to bring harmony into life's discords. And when the time comes for our departure, we'll rejoice with Peter's wife and ministry wives down through the ages. For you see, the rewards for faithful, unswerving commitment in all circumstances are out of this world.

When You've Been Hurt

"You know, I could handle all of the things that happened at our last church so much better if they had said those unkind things about *me*. But it hurt me so much to see my husband's pain. He's such a good pastor, and he just didn't deserve what they did to him. Some of the leaders wanted things to change and felt that they couldn't accomplish their goals under my husband's ministry. You wouldn't believe some of the letters he received. I didn't even show him some of the ones that were mailed to the house for him. He just didn't need any more pain. Our new church is great, and the people are wonderful. But I wonder if I can really trust them. My husband seems to have been able to put it all behind him. But to be perfectly honest, I'm still struggling. What can I do?"

I listened as Marjorie recounted her pain. It was a blessing to tell her about the promises in Isa. 43:18-19. "Forget the former things; do not dwell on the past. See, I am doing a new thing. Now it springs up; do you not perceive it? I am making a way in the desert and streams in the wasteland." I was glad to reassure her that our Father is still the Great Physician, who can also heal our broken hearts.

Vonette Bright and her husband, Bill, cofounded Campus

She Can't Even Play the Piano!

Crusade for Christ in 1951 and worked together as a great team until his death in July 2003. Over the course of those years they encountered many challenges and obstacles. There were times of pain and hurt when things did not always go smoothly. She shares about our Great Physician's willingness to heal our hurts and set us free:

You too can release a debt owed to you and be set free.

- First, acknowledge that you've been hurt. Be very specific about the injustice. Write it down.
- Second, determine what that person owes you. What do you want from her? This is where a lot of people create false expectations, and it really helps to define what you want. Write that down.
- Third, honestly consider the likelihood that you'll never get paid, that you'll never get what you want.

Then, finish by writing these words at the bottom: "Paid in full. Debt retired."

Let the debt go. Say, "I'm not going to require justice here. The debt that is owed me is gone. I've been forgiven that, and I'm not going to take that debt back."

That's heart surgery! The process may hurt and take time, but it's definitely worth the effort. You will be free indeed.

—Vonette Bright

From Vonette Bright, *My Heart in His Hands: Set Me Free Indeed* (Orlando, Fla.: New Life Publications, 2001), 32-33. Permission for reprint granted by Vonette Bright.

There are some practical steps to take when criticism comes our way. Carolyn Roper and her husband, David, pastored for 34 years in local church ministry. They are the founding directors of Idaho Mountain Ministries, a support and encouragement ministry to pastoral couples. This is what Carolyn has to say about healing hurts:

Many of us have used the familiar response to playground taunting, "Sticks and stones may break my bones, but words will never hurt me." That wasn't true on the playground, and it's still not true today. Many times, verbal barbs can hurt worse than stones. They can actually hurt more when they are being thrown at our loved ones.

There's no doubt that all of us who are involved in ministry will undergo criticism. That comes with the job description. So many times we find ourselves criticized unfairly, and many times it seems that we have no way to defend ourselves or respond. In addition, it is extremely painful when we are lambasted by people who are least qualified. Much of their ammunition comes from incomplete or erroneous information. It is not unusual for our strongest critics to be sinfully flawed individuals who have no real right to speak. Yet they can cause us much grief.

Our critics often attack our character and motives with absolutely no basis for their accusations. It would be wonderful if they approached us with love and concern, but many times they are vague and harsh. When they say unkind things to us and our spouses, we need to have a plan in place so that we can address and handle the pain. The following are some ways that we can bear up under criticism.

To Do for Yourself

- Examine your heart

It is essential that we take time to make sure of our thoughts and feelings. What is our response? Are we angry, frightened, resentful, or worried? It is important to pinpoint our reactions.

- Pray with openhearted transparency

We would do well to follow Christ's model as He prayed in the Garden. Be open before God as you pour out your heart. Take your anxiety and pain to the Lord first, and He will calm your heart. Then you can share with your husband. Remember that God is in control.

- Find a safe person

Look for a confidant who will listen and pray with you as you are totally honest with that person. Some of the best ones may be half a continent away!

- Be real

When the time is right, be totally candid and open with your spouse. Be careful not to allow your inner struggle to adversely affect your marriage.

To Do for Your Husband

- Be available

Make sure that you set aside everything else when your husband is ready to share. Be careful to guard against allowing the criticism to dominate your lives.

- Listen

Too many times we tend to jump into the conversation with opinions or fixes. Make sure any advice is appropriate and welcome.

- Be honest

If you believe that the criticism is valid, ask God to open your husband's heart to see the truth. Then your gentle words can lead to change and mistakes can be corrected. Encourage him to find a confidant.

- Lovingly express your concern

Simply saying, "I care, and I love you" lets your husband know you are a loyal friend who will be there regardless of what happens.

- Affirm your husband

Point out the fact that God chose him. Also, remind him that he has unique God-given gifts and qualities. Remind him of past victories. Be sure to be honest. Nothing warms the heart like sincere affirmation.

- Remain loyal

Direct critics to your husband. Don't listen to those who are determined to undermine his ministry. Rather than trying to reason with them, ask them to go directly to your husband (Matt. 18:15).

- Never give up hope

It is true that we grow most through the hard times. When we have been driven to our knees there are great benefits that come from kneeling together before the Lord. Together we can always know that God surely has a "future hope" for us (Prov. 23:18).

—Carolyn Roper

Adapted from Carolyn Roper, "When People Throw Stones," *Just Between Us,* summer 2003, 18.

In my previous book, *Unshakable Faith for Shaky Times,* Carol Rhoads wrote about committed faith—staying on course even during the tough times. In ministry, stress and continuous demands are a way of life—an occupational hazard. Hurtful situations happen. It's the nature of ministry. Ministry families can be fragmented by the 24/7 demands and the painful things that may occur. Carol addresses those issues:

⸙

For the first 18 years of our marriage, Ross was an evangelist, and we were thrilled with the joys of seeing many people come to a saving knowledge of Christ. When Ross began to pastor a church, I soon came to realize the pressures of being responsible as the pastor's wife to that group of people. It soon became obvious that this calling would be a great way to grow my faith! I must say that it was a blessing and privilege to serve as a pastor's wife for more than 20 years.

It's true that the life of a pastor's wife is more difficult than most people can imagine. Only a woman of strong faith who's wholly committed to God and the ministry can possibly cope with the pressures. Loneliness, insecurity, struggles, and overwhelming feelings of helplessness are constant challenges.

Perhaps the most difficult thing I faced was hearing undeserved criticism about my husband. Some was constructive, but there were instances when mean-spirited people who were jealous gossiped and hurt us deeply. Without our faith and ironclad commitment that we continue to reaffirm daily, we would most certainly have given up. Living in the glass walls of a parsonage was a constant challenge. But our strong faith in God and commitment sustained us, enabling us to stay close to the Lord and to each other.

Another thing I had to learn was how to balance the needs of church versus family. As our children grew and the church grew, the demands on me increased at home and at church. Ross encouraged me to seek God's wisdom concerning how I would divide my time and responsibilities. He never pressured me to do what was "expected."

I lived victoriously as a pastor's wife because of my faith in God and His faithfulness to me. My personal commitment and disciplined spiritual life sustained me through the toughest times. Because I have this solid foundation, I've been protected from Satan's attacks of self-pity and discouragement.

One of my favorite verses is found in Eph. 6:10: "Be strong in the Lord, and in the power of His might" (KJV). Today I can say with great confidence that my commitment is stronger than ever. And my faith is unwavering, regardless of the difficulties and challenges I face. God is always faithful, and it's a joy to serve Him.

—Carol Rhoads

My husband, Gene, along with a number of other pastors, has had the privilege of being part of filming nine prime-time television specials in Israel and other lands of the Bible. I have been so blessed to get to accompany him on five of those trips. One day when we were getting ready to enter the Catacombs in Rome, I noticed a marble statue of a lovely reclining young teenage girl. When I asked my guide who she was, she related a story that encourages my heart every time I reflect on it.

She said that beautiful teenager had been arrested along with her family during the intense persecution of the Early Church in Rome. Emperor Nero had ordered that everyone who refused to acknowledge him as god would be tortured and thrown to the hungry lions in the Coliseum. The vicious, gory deaths of those early believers were part of the "entertainment" for the spectators in the stands evening after evening. Sometimes soldiers were ordered to coat their captives in tar and place them on the stands where the torches stood. Then as twilight fell over the arena, they ignited the tar, and the martyrs became human torches as they burned to death.

When the day came and the soldiers arrived at the prison to take her family away, they told her, "You are so beautiful we are not going to take you to the lions today. We have plans for you. Nero might even want you!" That young girl watched with tears of great sorrow and agony as her family was led away, and she reached for them and cried out to be allowed to go with them. But the soldiers had their orders to hold back beautiful young girls, and they restrained her. That evening she could hear the roaring lines and the howling mob as all of her family died horrifying deaths because of their faith.

Day after day the soldiers came. They would say, "All you have to do to be saved from the lions is to recant your faith. Just say 'Nero is god.' It's that simple." Through the agony of her grief for her family without wavering at all, she always replied, "Jesus is Lord of my life."

Finally the day came when the soldiers said, "This is your last chance. You must acknowledge Nero as god today, or you will be thrown to the hungry lions tonight." To emphasize their point, they said, "Listen. Even now you can hear their roars. You know that they are starving. They will tear you apart. You will die a slow, agonizing death. Don't you remember that we told you how your family died? Just say those simple words, and you'll live. You'll have a good life." Then one more time they said, "Can't you hear the lions?"

With the glow of her love for Jesus shining in her eyes, she replied, "I will never renounce my faith in Jesus. He is the Lord of my life. Yes. I can hear the lions." Then she paused, and with a radiant smile illuminating her face, she said, "Oh, but can't you hear the *angels?*"

Then they led her off to her death. Another victory for Jesus!

As ministry wives, so many times we're tempted to hear the roaring of the lions rather than sense the presence of our Father's care and protection around us. I love Heb. 12:1-3: "Since we are surrounded by such a great cloud of witnesses, let us throw off everything that hinders us and the sin that so easily entangles, and let us run with perseverance the race marked out for us. Let us fix our eyes on Jesus, the author and perfecter of our faith, who for the joy set before him endured the cross, scorning its shame, and sat down at the right hand of the throne of God. Consider him who endured such opposition from sinful men, so that you will not grow weary and lose heart."

I challenge you, dear ministry sister—don't lose heart! We can still find victory in Jesus. Our loving Heavenly Father will give us the grace to overcome the roaring lions (even if they may be board members or deacons!) as we listen for the still small voice. Our Good Shepherd has promised to keep us. We read in Ps. 91:11-12, "He will command His angels concerning you to guard you in all your ways; they will lift you up in their hands, so that you will not strike your foot against a stone."

Remember—on the days when the lions are roaring, His angels are standing guard. Be sure you're listening to the gentle whisper.

Powerful Prayer Strategies

I must confess that one of the most difficult aspects of my walk with the Lord is being still—and listening. One of my heroes has always been Mother Teresa. An interviewer once commented to her, "I've read that you pray a lot. What do you do when you pray?"

She replied, "I listen."

Then he asked, "And what does God do?"

Her answer is classic: "He listens."

Oh, Lord—how I want to be a better listener!

Patsy Lewis is a veteran ministry wife who has developed powerful prayer and listening strategies. She, too, has learned the incredible rewards that come through listening to His still, small voice. Anyone could use these awesome plans to expand quiet times and prayer ministries.

I was tucking Kevin in bed late one Sunday evening when he was barely four and Lanissa was a tiny baby. What a day it had been! I had gotten up early, taught Sunday School and children's church, had guests for lunch, did a Bible study with a couple of new Christians, went to a special choir practice, came home from the evening service, fed my family, and still hadn't finished washing the lunch dishes.

Kevin asked me to read a Bible story to him. My reply was "My throat's too sore." And it was. After we both prayed, he pulled my face down to his cheek, hugged me tightly, and whispered, "I love you, Mommy." Then he said, "Let's talk." I pulled away and replied, "I can't. I have to finish washing dishes." He quickly inquired, "Well, when can we talk?" I responded, "Maybe tomorrow," as I turned out his bedroom light.

I finished washing the dishes and fell wearily into bed after midnight. In the wee morning hours I was awakened with that dialog ringing in my ears. I began to wonder how long he might have waited just to talk. Tomorrow he could assume I was again too busy, or suppose by some tragedy there would be no chance to talk tomorrow. Then I thought, *What if God said that to me in a time of dire need?*

It wasn't long until I *was* in a state of dire need. My husband was away in ministry for long hours. Since we had only one car, I was housebound days at a time with a preschooler and a very active toddler who rarely slept and could outrun me. With all of my activities—plus ill health—I began praying for a physical touch and changes in my attitude and behavior. Nothing seemed to be happening.

In my despair I told God and my husband I wasn't sure prayer worked; therefore, I was no longer going to pray. In spite of my resolve, I still found myself talking to God but realized I was giving Him all the advice. Finally I decided to stop telling God how to fix me. Instead, I asked Him for answers and began to listen. He revealed truths to me about me, and I became eager to hear what He had to say. Eventually the Holy Spirit led me on a prayer walk starting with my earliest recollections. I prayed through my life year by year until a wonderful healing of memories took place. I reached a new freedom in my relationship with God.

As a result of this experience and other circumstances, I began to keep a prayer journal in a spiral notebook and recorded

- My questions and His answers;
- Prayer requests and praises;
- Prayers from my heart and doubts in my thoughts;
- Highlights from my spiritual journey and creative ideas.

I discovered that

- Simple prayers work.
- We can tell God our fears, doubts, worries, concerns, anything.
- When we listen, we can hear Him speak.

As my prayer life grew, I felt led to begin Potter's Clay Ministries for hurting people who long to reach their potential. My mission statement became "to encourage discovery and enlighten hearts by offering a legacy of hope to those God places in my path." I have seen many lives transformed and freed by this prayer-filled journey for the healing of memories and through small prayer groups and retreats.

Three prayer strategies I've used extensively in recent years include organizing overnight prayer retreats, developing a corporate prayer team, and expanding my personal prayer times.

Overnight Prayer Retreats. I frequently host these prayer retreats in my home or at retreat centers for groups of four to six ladies to pray for our children. We laugh together, cry together, eat together, and return home invigorated by our time of prayer for our families. I keep the plan uncomplicated and the food simple. When each lady arrives, she's given a copy of Stormie Omartian's book *The Power of a Praying Parent*. Then we proceed through the following steps:

- We establish and discuss a confidentiality rule.
- We draw names to see who goes first and start with that person's oldest child.
- Before praying, the mother shares a picture and brief story about the child.
- We limit talking and give maximum prayer time by presenting requests as we pray.
- We pray silently with each mother, asking for discernment in how to pray for her child.
- One or two others pray for that son or daughter.
- Sometimes a mother who is shy about praying aloud will read a prayer.
- We claim a Bible verse for the child and pray that promise.

While we're together, we often plan additional small prayer groups in shorter sessions to pray for our children and grandchildren at the beginning of the school year. We plan prayer walks with one or two partners to pray for our children during the walk, and we plan times to pray together for our husbands. We choose two prayer partners, and each gives the name of a person for whom she is praying. We then plan to meet weekly or use three-way calling to pray for the three prayer requests. We agree to intercede for one another throughout the week in our private prayers. Remember—there's power in praying together. Read Matt. 18:19-20.

Corporate Prayer Teams. Recently my daughter called to tell me about the Oklahoma Concert of Prayer.

She explained that individuals in each county commit to a specific hour each month to pray for needs in that state. The goal is to have each county fill every hour of every day of the month.

I had asked God for a prayer strategy for the churches in my state of Kentucky, and I believe this was an answer to my prayer. I enlisted the help of my husband, who is the district superintendent of our denomination. We mailed a letter to the pastors on our district requesting that they help enlist people to pray for one hour each month for ministries across our district. We outlined the plan to have someone praying at all times and suggested a day of the month and cluster of hours for their churches.

I mailed the letter at 2:00 P.M., and before noon the next day I received a fax with the first response. That particular church had been given 11 hours and every hour was filled. The next response came from a small church that had been asked to fill only four hours. The pastor wrote, "We accept the prayer challenge, but we would like to cover the full day." His letter listed 24 names of individuals committed to praying.

We send a prayer suggestion guide to prayer team members at the beginning of each month to be used as a teaching tool on prayer for the more than 800 prayer team members we now have.

Ask God to give you a special prayer strategy for your church, or adapt this idea. God will give you a creative plan that works.

Expand Personal Prayer Time: Nothing takes the place of daily personal talks with God, but if you're like me, you may have found that you're doing more talking than listening. A few years ago I challenged myself to listen to God for 10 minutes without interrupting Him.

She Can't Even Play the Piano!

With notebook and pen in hand, I set a timer and sat down at the table. Among other things that I wrote during that first listening time was the unexpected instruction to call the piano tuner. I obeyed, and as a result of my obedience God began giving me songs through scripture as I listened to Him. After writing more than 200 scripture-songs, I realized that God had honored my desire to pray and memorize more scripture.

I've continued these listening times, and God has revealed amazing truths to me. Because of what I have learned through my listening prayers, I often give prayer journals to friends, and I always include the following requests:

- Get out of bed 10 minutes earlier each day.
- Listen quietly for what God has to say to you.
- Even if you don't sense His speaking to you, sit in His presence and enjoy His peace.
- Record in this journal anything He may say to you.
- When your journal is filled, call me and share with me what's going on in your life.

The message God shares with you will be His special gift—uniquely personal to you.

The Lord has continued to reveal ways to enhance my personal prayer life. Here are some ideas that you might incorporate into your time with the Lord:

- Pray scripture, and turn Bible passages into prayers.
- Sing songs of praise, or speak the lyrics of a hymn.
- Take a prayer walk through your home.

Use a family photo album as a tool for prayer, and pray God's blessing on each person in the album; give thanks for gifts and treasures in your home; pray for those who have given gifts that are displayed in your home; ask God to permeate each room with His blessed Holy Spirit; remove anything that is not godly—books, pictures, videos.

Even though you may not have a talent for playing the piano or speaking to large groups or writing or singing or _____ (you fill in the blank), you can talk to God in prayer and invite others to pray with you. As you quiet your heart to hear what God has to say to you, you might hear Him whispering to you as my son whispered to me 30 years ago, *I love you. Let's talk.* And your response can be, *Yes, Lord. Speak to me, for I'm listening.*

—Patsy Lewis

Several years ago I was invited to speak about prayer in several venues. I confess that I felt very inadequate. As I studied and prayed about prayer, I pondered about where our prayers go. Within minutes the Lord led me to Rev. 5:6-8. I was so blessed that I had to leave the house and walk around the lake as the glory of how much our Father cherishes our prayers was revealed to me. When I returned home He gave this poem to me:

Where Do Our Prayers Go?
(Rev. 5:6-8)

My heart was heavy burdened
As I bowed there by my bed,
Recalling a lifetime of prayers
And countless tears I'd shed.

She Can't Even Play the Piano!

I cried out from my heart,
　　"Lord, where do my prayers go?
I know you hear them all,
　　For the Bible tells me so."

Then my eyes fell on the pages,
　　And your Word to me was shown.
Hope swelled within as I read,
　　"Your prayers are kept here by my throne.

"For no prayer is ever wasted;
　　I keep them in bowls made of gold.
They're the very fragrance of heaven;
　　Their aroma can never be told.

"That precious pungent perfume
　　Is the essence that does pervade
The halls and streets of my city,
　　Gathered each time that you pray."

My heart was filled with gladness
　　At that scene before the throne.
Our Father collects our prayers
　　To perfume His heavenly home!

To think that the sacred scent
　　Drifting on the heavenly breeze
Flows there from the faithful saints
　　Who spend time with Him on their knees.

All of the prayers that we pray
　　Fly straight to that heavenly realm.
They're the aroma in the nostrils of God
　　In the throne room of the Lamb!

Pray Together; Stay Together

When I think of mighty prayer warriors, the first person I think of is Vonette Bright. It was such a joy to meet and interview her and her dear husband, Bill, in Amsterdam in 2000. Within moments of being with her, I immediately sensed that I was in the presence of an awesome woman of God. Her gracious kindness and caring tender spirit exude His love. For years I had read about her prayer ministry that was their source of inspiration and strength that undergirded everything they undertook. How fitting and blessed it is for us to have this precious ministry wife to share words of wisdom and insight on the awesome power of prayer in the lives of ministry couples!

⟡

Working in ministry is challenging, yet fulfilling. Nothing is more crucial in the life of a husband and wife in service to our Lord than a consistent and meaningful prayer life—both as a couple and as individuals. How I thank God that He impressed upon Bill and me and our volunteers the importance of prayer when our ministry was first organized! I can't imagine where we would be today if we hadn't established a priority of prayer.

The first year that Bill and I lived near the UCLA campus, we organized a continuous prayer chain by dividing twenty-four hours into ninety-six 15-minute periods. Volunteers from all over the country signed up to pray during a particular 15-minute time slot. That year we saw 250 students respond to the gospel of Jesus Christ.

Later, as the ministry grew, we began to have a great concern for our nation, which led us to a united prayer effort called the Great Commission Prayer Crusade. This ministry, which I had the privilege of directing, was born to particularly give women throughout the nation a united opportunity to influence our country's moral and spiritual values.

As I look back on the ministry of the Great Commission Prayer Crusade, I remember that we saw amazing answers to prayer. In one city, a teenage girl was kidnapped. What agony that caused! After three long weeks of searching, many people gave her up for dead. But others were still united in prayer for that city, and she was returned unharmed and unmolested.

When the Vietnam War ended, thousands of refugees fled to South Vietnam. They were housed in refugee camps until sponsors were found to help them settle in a new homeland. Thousands of Christians prayed for the physical and spiritual needs of the refugees. Our Campus Crusade for Christ director and his wife were missing persons for four years. We never ceased praying for their safety. After reaching a refugee camp in Thailand, he was able to make contact with us. In December 1975 the refugee camps were closed, because the remaining refugees had located sponsors. Of the 131,000 displaced Vietnamese people, more than 80,000 found sponsors through church-related groups. God does answer prayer.

As you can see, our prayer efforts covered larger issues as well as those of a personal nature. Through this, I learned that God is both intimate and universal. Nothing is too small or too large for Him to handle. Today, in my personal life as well as in the ministry of Campus Crusade, prayer is top priority.

Tragically, Christians are often misinformed about the role of prayer. God speaks to us through His Word, but to cultivate this relationship we communicate with God through prayer. Unfortunately, the prayers of countless people never go beyond *Now I lay me down to sleep* or *God bless the missionaries*. Many pray only in emergencies or fail to pray because they don't feel worthy enough to approach God. Have you ever found yourself in one of these categories?

Prayer is so important that Jesus found it necessary to pray often, and by His words and His example He taught His disciples to pray. People through whom God accomplished much have relied on prayer for wisdom and power.

The following are some of the Bible's principles on the importance of prayer in our lives:

- We are to pray without ceasing (1 Thess. 5:17). We can talk to God hundreds of times throughout our day. No matter is too insignificant to bring to His attention or too difficult for His power.
- God will show us remarkable secrets when we call on Him (Jer. 33:3). He will reveal mysteries to us that we did not know.
- We don't have because we don't ask (James 4:2). God is waiting to answer our prayers, but we fail

to acknowledge that we need His help, so we suffer the consequences.

- We will experience abundant joy through prayer (John 16:24). If you have ever seen God answer your desperate plea in His miraculous ways, you know what this verse is promising.

Developing a Prayer Life

Some simple steps can help you develop a lifestyle of prayer. I encourage you to keep a notebook in which you record prayer requests, the date answered, and your praises and thanksgiving to God. Keep your list with your devotional material so you'll use it every day.

Your list will perform three functions for you. First, it will remind you of requests, praises, and thanks that you need to offer to God.

Second, it will help you keep your praises, thanksgiving, and requests balanced so that you don't become a "gimme" Christian and neglect giving God the honor and gratitude He deserves. You can use your date answered column as part of your thanksgiving list.

Third, recording answers to prayer will encourage you in your walk with God. How many times have you prayed for something, received an answer, but forgotten you had even asked God for it? That happens to all of us if we're not careful to acknowledge His role in our lives. Recording requests and the date answered will help you avoid this omission. And when you are tempted to be discouraged because it doesn't seem God is answering a specific request, you can look back to see how God has worked in your behalf in the past. Our confidence in God grows, He becomes more real to us, and our faith is strengthened as we communicate in an intimate relationship with our Heavenly Father.

Your prayer list will also help you to pray specifically. By His example and teaching, Jesus encourages us to present God with specific requests—those that have to do with our needs, our relationships, or anything that concerns us. If we do not ask specifically, how can we expect God to answer specifically?

God delights in listening to us express our desires to Him. Prayers do not have to be long, nor does a person need to be super-spiritual to talk to God. He just wants us to pour our hearts out to Him so that He can heal, soothe, and deal with our inner needs. He reveals himself to us as we see His power in action in our behalf. Never be afraid to bring your deepest desires to Him, because He always handles them with utmost care. You may want to use a journal to write out prayers to God in which you express your desires.

Find your own special times and places to pray. It is not necessary to be in any particular position to pray. I find some of my greatest times of communication with the Lord are when I'm working with my hands and my mind is free to concentrate on talking to Christ. God wants to be a part of the pattern of your life!

But do allot time. I find the best time to talk to God and read the Bible is first thing in the morning. That timing helps you begin your day in the right attitude and in the power of the Spirit.

For this reason, Bill and I established the habit of praying together before getting out of bed in the morning. This practice was invaluable to us in keeping our communication open with God and with each other. You can't pray with someone if there is conflict between you. Therefore, we talked out our differences, making sure we had heard each other. We also established praying together at night before going to bed. We would go to bed in love and awaken the same way the next morning.

The Battle Is the Lord's

I must warn you that developing a consistent, faith-based prayer life is a constant battle. Though we must be prepared for spiritual conflict, we must also remember that our battle is the Lord's. Read this warning from God to an Old Testament king who faced an overwhelming enemy: "Listen, King Jehoshaphat! Listen, all you people of Judah and Jerusalem! This is what the LORD says: Do not be afraid! Don't be discouraged by this mighty army, for the battle is not yours, but God's" (2 Chron. 20:15, NLT).

Why is this life sometimes so difficult and challenging to live? The greatest reason for the difficulties we face each day is just a lack of understanding about who God is. Yes, we make choices that can create problems, and these are of our own doing, but when we surrender our lives to Him, our response to the consequences can be controlled by God. The purpose of prayer is to experience an intimate relationship with God in the person of Jesus Christ. The more I pray, the more I wonder why I do not pray more. The benefits are more rewarding than any other way I spend my time.

Remember: you received Christ Jesus as Lord by faith. That is how you must pray—by faith. Don't fight the spiritual battle alone. Count on God. Step over the threshold and experience real, true joy. Make your conversations with those that count.

—Vonette Bright

Adapted from Vonette Zachary Bright, *The Woman Within: Discover the Joy of Life in Christ* (Orlando, Fla.: New Life Publications), 167-81. Used by permission.

How wonderful to go to bed in love and to awaken in love the next morning! Gene and I call those "bookend moments." And we've found that whatever happens between those bookends—whether good or not so good—is overshadowed by our prayers and love, because we know we're held in our Father's embrace.

Maintaining Joy
The Delight of Serving and Being Served

Have fun in the parsonage. Does that sound like an oxymoron? Is it possible to laugh and find real joy inside glass walls? Yes, it is. I loved it when I read that Chuck and Cynthia Swindoll ride motorcycles. The picture of them together is priceless—worth more than a thousand words.

Recently Gene and I were speaking at a church in Junction City, Kansas, on a Sunday morning. It was such a blessing to observe the exuberant and genuine joy that the beautiful young pastor's wife, Deb Dryness, was experiencing as part of the worship team. Her husband, Brad, was hiking Pike's Peak with their son Dan. Deb and their recently adopted son, Greg, were eager for them to return to hear all about their trip. That morning she emanated her love for Jesus and her delight in serving Him as she fell to her knees in heartfelt worship.

At lunch afterwards, I commented on how touched we were by the pure joy she reflected in her ministry assignment.

I knew a little about some issues with which she was dealing. Yet Deb radiated with her love for Jesus. I asked her, "How do you sustain the joy of ministry with all the challenges you face daily?" Her eyes sparkled as she answered, "I stay in the Word and on my knees. And then Brad and I take time for each other and to do the things that we really enjoy—like hiking Pike's Peak. Just when I need it most, the Lord always gives me just what I must have to keep the faith. I just love what I'm doing!" I must say that my heart swelled with her contagious joy.

Unfortunately, too many ministry couples get so caught up in the challenges, assignments, and responsibilities that they take too little time to have real fun. Gene says often that nobody has ever enjoyed life more than he does. He has learned the value of finding what brings joy and laughter into his life and then doing just that.

An evangelist's wife from the East Coast confided in me one day that she could not remember the last time she and her husband had relaxed and laughed together. She said, "We're together all the time as we travel from assignment to assignment. We look really good when we're up front laughing and cutting up. But when we get into our car to head home or to the next engagement, we hardly seem able to talk to each other, let alone have real fun."

Tears bubbled over as she spoke. When I asked her how long it had been since they had been on a date, she looked at me as though she didn't understand the question. Then she said, "We haven't had a date since our wedding day."

The best advice I could give her was to have Gene talk to her husband. The next day after the morning service, Gene played golf with him. I don't know what Gene told her husband, but a couple of days later, I caught them giggling as they walked through the woods behind our cabins holding hands. It was beautiful to behold!

So how do we have fun in the spotlight of ministry? There are many ways.

- Have a date at least once a week. Make that a time when you don't talk about problems or ministry but just hang out together.
- Participate in each other's hobbies. I'm not a golfer, but occasionally I'll walk the course with Gene or drive the golf cart for him.
- Surprise each other with special notes or unexpected treats. Gene plants rose bushes for me. He leaves a rose-bud on the kitchen counter in a vase when they're blooming. I love to leave notes for him and small gifts. Once when he was going to be away on Valentine's Day, I tucked a gift of boxers with hearts on them into his suitcase. He was rooming with one of the staff guys. It was hilarious when he put them on. When the lights went out, he discovered that the hearts glowed in the dark. He's still hearing about that one!
- Plan a romantic getaway—just the two of you—when possible. Just spending the night at Motel 6 and enjoying the continental breakfast can spice up your lives.
- Compliment each other. Pastor your minister husband. Create a safe haven—a refuge for him.

Gene says, "Happy husbands have happy wives who have happy husbands and on and on . . ." Remember: when Mama's happy, everybody's happy.

Not long ago I was talking with Teresa Eller, a pastor's wife who has discovered some secrets to happiness for ministry couples. Here's what she said,

I've come to realize that joy in the ministry journey can be obtained in three areas: personally, as a couple, and in ministry—all of equal importance. Discouragement can seep in if any area is neglected.

Personal Joy

We can't share what we don't have. The joy of the Lord spreads to others as they witness your inner joy. Being grounded in the Lord through daily personal devotions and prayer is a key factor in sustaining that joy.

God is my personal confidant. I tell Him everything. I take all my concerns straight to the one who knows all about it and will do something about it. He loves me regardless of what I say to Him, and His love never wavers. He can and will change hearts, marriages, and lives. What I've found so many times is that mostly He changes me instead of my circumstances.

The title "minister's wife" represents a person and not a job description. Being true to myself the way God created me brings more joy than trying to be someone I'm not. Rather than trying to be everything to everyone, I try to be open to God's will and do what the Lord says. Many times that means getting alone with God and seeking His plan.

Friends and family—even our husbands—may try to tell us what we ought to do. It's important to prayerfully consider those requests. A church member once asked me to pray about being a children's Sunday School teacher. As I prayed, it became clear that teaching children was not the Lord's will for me at that time. That person was not happy with me. After all, since I was the pastor's wife, I should be willing to do anything that was asked of me, right? Because I knew God had given me an answer about the matter, I was able to gently say no to the request and sustain my personal joy and peace.

Of course, we do need to be open and pliable and

willing to fill in wherever needed, at least on a temporary basis. But I try to be sure that my long-term ministries are those to which the Lord has called me and in areas in which He has gifted me.

Just about every ministry wife has taken on all kinds of jobs in the church to fill various needs. But we must be careful not to step in and take over apart from the Lord's will, because He may be dealing with someone else He wants to fill that position. Give that person a chance to answer God's call. We find our greatest personal joy and fulfillment by working in those areas in which the Lord has gifted us.

Joy as a Couple

It's easy to get caught up in ministry and neglect our own marriages. Finding ways to have fun together may sometimes seem difficult, but it's not impossible.

A few years ago my husband was very busy. It seemed he was in charge of everything at church. In addition, we were running fast to keep up with our children's activities. I began to feel neglected; it seemed that he had time for everyone but me. To be honest, I was feeling sorry for myself. I wanted his attention—just a little bit of his time. Loneliness is not uncommon for many pastors' wives. Pastors are almost always busy. Sometimes it's a struggle not to feel neglected and isolated.

I decided one day that we were going to make time to talk when he came home that evening. When he walked through the door, I said, "Dan, I need to talk to you".

He said, "Sure—just follow me around the house while I put these things away."

I said in a loud voice, "I will not follow you around the house. Stop right now and look at me!"

I began to cry. When I finally stopped crying, I began to share my heart with him. I told him we needed time together—alone.

He was very loving and kind as he listened. When I finished, he said, "I'm in charge of so many things, I can't arrange one more thing. But if you plan something, I'll show up." That night we decided to set aside a regular date night every week.

We've been having that date night for a few years now. Dan insists that he looks forward to it more than I do. (Not really!) We've done many things together that bring both of us joy in our marriage. It's a good example for the couples in our congregation as well. How can we help our people find joy in their marriages if we don't model that for them?

When we hear couples in our congregation say that they don't have time or money, we have a few a suggestions about how they can spend time alone. Dates can be inexpensive or expensive, ranging from a picnic in the park to a steak dinner at a fancy restaurant.

Make a list of things that you and your husband enjoy doing. Write each of them on separate pieces of paper. Put them in a jar, and shake it. Then take turns planning your special date.

Draw from your stash of ideas. If you think of something you would like to do, write it down and add it to your collection. The important thing is that you spend time together. On our date nights we make it a practice not to talk about church, kids, or work. We focus on each other, our dreams, and our future as a couple.

Joy in Serving

I've experienced great joy in ministering to others. At Christmastime I enjoy remembering those who serve us all year. When I drive up to my favorite fast-food restaurants, I hand out gifts of homemade goodies and say, "This is to say thanks to you." I attach a note that simply reads, *Thank you for serving me every day. God bless you. Homemade especially for you.*

I once took homemade candy to a grumpy donut shop attendant. You should have seen her face light up. It made my heart jump with joy. I learned a few weeks later that her father had left the family and her mother had cancer. The young girl was pregnant, and the baby's father had stepped out of the picture. No wonder she was grumpy! It was a joy to show Christ's love to her through candy.

I was chatting with a parishioner about his upcoming 20th wedding anniversary. When I asked him what he was going to do for the big day, he responded. "Oh, nothing. We've been married so long we don't bother with that anymore."

My jaw dropped in disbelief. After 20 years of marriage, there had to be a way for them to enjoy something special in spite of having little money and two kids at home. I decided that this couple needed intervention, and I set my plan in motion.

I let a week go by. Then I telephoned them to tell them that I was planning a dinner party for couples and that children were not invited. If they wanted to attend, it must be both of them.

What I really called to find out was what kind of food they liked, and as the conversation progressed, the wife gave me all the information I needed to make this celebration a success.

On the designated evening our friends came to our house as arranged, expecting a house full of people. What they discovered was a private candlelight dining experience. When they arrived, Dan and I were dressed in formal clothes. Dan announced them as though there were a hundred people in the room. We seated them in a special room that was prepared just for them.

With soft music playing in the background, we began the meal with a blessing and a reading from the *Couples' Devotional Bible*. We encouraged them to focus on each other—to talk about how they met, when they first fell in love, and what attracted them to each other. For us, the real fun happened in the kitchen while preparing to serve each course. Dan and I had a ball as we laughed, kissed, and felt the presence of God in a very real way.

At the conclusion of the meal, we picked up the couple's children and brought them back to our home for a slumber party. Since they could not afford a special evening at a luxurious hotel, we provided a night alone for them—in their own home. The evening was a success, not only for them but also for us. We still tease each other about which couple had more fun.

It's true that God uses anything that we make available. As ministry wives, we work for the Lord not just at church but everywhere we go. We can spread His joy and receive His joy in return.

Joy comes from noticing and acting upon the little things in life. When we treat each area of our lives as a priority, set aside for the Master's use, we'll be overcome with joy.

—Teresa Eller

There's no doubt that the servant's heart is a happy heart. The essence of ministry is giving to the lost, hurting, and needy around us, yet crises and distresses come into the parsonage as well. One of the perks of ministry is to feel the loving support of our people banding around us during times of heartache and pain. The truth is that when those of us who are in ministry experience a crisis, God gives us access to a large group of prayer warriors who join us in the battle as they bombard heaven for us. And can those ladies cook!

Casseroles, cakes, compassion, and caring concern surround us in our times of illness, loss, and heartache. As a matter of fact, we experience role reversal during times of distress when our people pastor their pastor. Linda Toler shares about the blessing of receiving loving care from parishioners.

I was three and a half weeks away from delivering our second child, and my doctor appointment was his last of the day. First, I saw our family doctor; then he walked me to the surgeon's office down the hall. Complications! They informed me that I would be entering the Fayette County Hospital within the hour, and a C-section would be scheduled for early the next morning.

Stan was speaking at a conference in Dayton, more than an hour away. His parents hurried down from Columbus, Ohio, and took me to the hospital, while Stan rushed home from Dayton. After a restless night for all of us, early the next morning—a Saturday—I was rolled into surgery. Suddenly I felt faint, and after a quick check of vitals, the anesthesiologist wasted no time putting me under. I had experienced the fainting spells several times before and had also fallen twice. A troubled pregnancy!

At 8:41 A.M. Adam James Toler entered the world prematurely—but what a whopper! He weighed 8 pounds and 10 ounces!

As the day wore on, friends came to support us, but all I could do was sleep. I remember friends like David and Connie Dean being in my room, talking to Stan, and praying with us. I seemed powerless to open my eyes or speak. No one realized I could hear everything that was said.

Our precious baby had been placed in an incubator. By evening the oxygen levels were being increased.

Early Sunday morning a pediatrician with a heavy accent woke me. He said, "Your baby is having some problems." Through the fog in my head I heard, "collapsed lung," "high oxygen levels," "stress on vital organs," "serious problem."

I called home and woke Stan. He rushed to the hospital where our precious Adam was awaiting transport in the neonatal intensive care mobile unit to Children's Hospital in Columbus.

After Adam was prepped for the trip, the transport team brought him to us. I held him for about two minutes—a brief bonding moment. I can't describe the deep ache as I let him go. Hearing the sirens wail as they drove away broke my heart. For at least the next two years I burst into tears at the sound of an ambulance siren.

Our emotional roller coaster was picking up speed. Stan hugged me as we cried, our tears mingled with the haunting thought that our son might not live through the day. Through tears, Stan said, "Linda, who pastors the pastor's family? After all these years of ministry, we've stood by and encouraged others. We've prayed prayers of comfort for many families, and here we are alone."

Stan tells me that I pulled him down close and prayed a beautiful prayer, thanking God for Adam and

boldly asking for a miracle. I distinctly remember reading in one of Barbara Johnson's books, "Sometimes God
calms the raging storm; sometimes He lets the storm
rage and calms the child."

In 2 Cor. 12:9 the Lord says, "My grace is sufficient
for thee: for my strength is made perfect in weakness"
(KJV). What a glorious promise!

Hours and days passed. Our church family graciously loved us and cared for us. Julia Dawson called hundreds of people in our community requesting prayer for
Adam. They conducted daily prayer vigils at the church
and visited us at the two hospitals. They arranged for
my parents to come from Georgia to Ohio to care for
our four-year-old son, Seth. They visited Adam and sup-
ported Stan at the Children's Hospital in Columbus.

These loving friends, our church family, visited me in
the Fayette County Hospital. As it turned out, I had
complications and couldn't join Stan and Adam. During
all their care-giving, we realized the importance of lay
ministry. We learned that laypersons can pastor the
pastor's family.

On day three, Adam took a turn for the worse.
Phone calls were made, and our church family prayed.
Hundreds gathered at our church, Heritage Memorial.
Friends from California to Virginia prayed. Heaven was
being bombarded for Adam James.

Hours later, Stan was allowed to see him. Stan told
me later, "He was laying on his tummy, no diaper, and
rear in the air."

The nurse said to Stan, "That's the butt sign. He is
going to make it. Your prayers have been answered."
And he did make it.

Ten years later, in a different town in a different
state and in a different church, we were reminded again

of who pastors the pastor's family. We had only been at Nashville First Church for five months when cancer came to call.

I was diagnosed with colon cancer the day before Thanksgiving, and the surgery was scheduled for less than a week later. Michael Santi, my physician, entered the hospital room smiling and sat beside me on the bed. After explaining the surgery and recuperation time, he took my hands and held them toward heaven. "Linda," he said, "tomorrow our hands will be in His hands." Then he added, *God, I cannot do this alone. I need Your help.* In the midst of our frightening situation, God gave us a Christian doctor.

I've always loved to decorate my home for Christmas, bake holiday treats, and entertain family and friends. But in 1991 my plans changed. I had always been concerned with "doing" to prove my worth, but I learned that "being" His and having His approval is what matters.

Once again we saw love at work. Families prayed for us, brought meals, visited, transported our sons to activities, did our laundry, cleaned our house, and even scrubbed our toilets.

Throughout our years in ministry, we've been encouraged to trust God through the changes of life in four simple ways:

- The prayers of God's people.
- The presence and support of family.
- A Christian doctor.
- Calls, visits, cards, letters, and acts of kindness of friends.

So when someone asks me, "Who pastors the pastor's family?" I know the answer!

—Linda Toler

Another way we can take joy in the ministry is by serving our mates. I love doing special things for Gene. It delights him and makes me happy when I surprise him with small gifts. A couple of years ago I started a miniature car collection for him, and he really enjoys those. Every time I give another one to him, his face lights up. When he is especially touched by something, he has a very special chuckle that tickles my heart-strings. I love to hear it.

I believe that Acts 20:24 sums up the essence of our goal in ministry: "None of these things move me, neither count I my life dear unto myself, so that I might *finish my course with joy*, and the ministry, which I have received of the Lord Jesus, to testify to the gospel of the grace of God" (KJV, emphasis added).

Early in his marriage to his late wife, Bettye, Gene began planting rose bushes that eventually became a beautiful rose garden for her. Many days as he was leaving in the morning, he picked a rose, stripped the thorns with his pocketknife, brought it back into the kitchen, and put it into a bud vase on the sink as a tangible reminder of his love for her while he was gone that day.

Gene told me about that custom as we were getting to know each other, and I found it to be very endearing as he showed me Bettye's rose garden. It was a riot of radiant colors and fragrant aromas wafting across the breeze. There was a perfect view of the garden from the kitchen window. When we were married and I moved into that house, I could see those roses all the time, and they brightened each day.

We had been married just a short while when roses began to appear on my kitchen counter. They brought me joy and warmed my heart throughout the day. Five years later when we moved into a new house, one of the first things Gene did was plant another rose garden. Day after day, I continue to find a beautiful bud blossoming on my kitchen counter. As a matter of fact, as I write this, the pungent perfume from a beautiful yellow rosebud permeates our living room. I was so touched by Gene's thoughtfulness that I wrote the following poem to thank him on our second Valentine's Day together. I thank God for my ministry husband who promised me a rose garden—and delivered!

A Rose for My Love

You bring to me a lovely rose,
Daily plucked as it brightly grows.
This pungent, glorious, floral gift
Always causes my heart to lift.

For it's more than just a lovely flower
As it sprinkles me with love's sweet shower.
It reminds me of the great measure
Of love we share—a priceless treasure.

Truly you are unique—that's very clear,
And that makes you so incredibly dear.
You fill my days, my world, my life
With the great joy of being your wife.

And that's why I had to say, dear one,
You made my life when my heart you won.
So I pledge my love afresh and anew
With this loving, rosy tribute to you.

Each of us has different "joy triggers." Obviously, stopping to smell the roses is one for Gene and me. Maybe, as with the Swindolls, your idea of fun is hopping onto the back of your husband's motorcycle and speeding down the highway. The challenge for every ministry couple is to find out what works for them both, hang on to each other for dear life, and then ride off into the sunset together—on motorcycles or whatever—wherever the Lord leads.

Leaving a Lasting Legacy 13

𝓘 remember my first junior choir practice. I was so excited. Our pastor's wife, Twylah Ellwanger, was wonderful. She and her husband, Bill, pastored my home church in Roanoke, Virginia. It was their first pastorate, and, as we say in the South, they jumped in "whole hog." They were an attractive, talented couple, and the whole congregation fell in love with them.

As we gathered for choir practice, the other children and I could hardly wait to see the music that Saturday morning and find out what junior choir was all about. My eight-year-old energy and enthusiasm were boiling. Sister Ellwanger, as we called her, taught us parts and helped me learn my alto range. Before long there were more than 30 kids singing their hearts out for our beautiful, loving pastor's wife. There were never too many practices in my opinion, and I always felt sad when it was time to leave.

We were especially excited one day when she announced, "We're going to have choir robes made so that you can all look alike." Wow! A real choir robe! Our good and faithful neighbor Beatrice Agnew made robes for my sister Jane and me as well as for several other choir members. She even sewed our names on a tag in the back.

Fifty-two years later, I still remember the joy of singing

with the other kids in the choir loft in front of the whole church. I kept that choir robe for more than 40 years as a treasured reminder of childhood memories.

There was nothing Sister Ellwanger couldn't do. She played the piano and organ beautifully. She and her husband sang together. She also started a teen choir, and they had outfits made as well.

I remember going to a chili dinner at the parsonage late one cold winter afternoon after a special choir practice. A fire roared in the fireplace, and it smelled so good. Everything was beautifully decorated, and I spent a lot of time walking around in wide-eyed wonder. To this day, I recall feeling so warm and welcome. And the chili was delicious.

My alto voice was mediocre, but I felt special singing in that choir—especially when our robes were ready. Our first performance in those short little blue robes with white collars and big black bows was a thrill. It was such fun to shake those floppy, triangle-shaped sleeves!

For four of my most formative years Pastor and Sister Ellwanger nurtured and cared for us. It didn't seem to matter to them at all that ours was a "blue collar" church in the inner city. They loved us and treated us as though we were uptown, educated professionals. It was during those years that I committed my life to the Lord.

Many of the things I learned and practice today reflect back to those four years of nurturing and unconditional love. Since that time, my goal has always been to express that same kind of unmitigated care and compassion for everyone I encounter regardless of his or her background and station in life.

I thank God for a pastor's wife who poured herself into our lives. No doubt we tried her patience and endurance. I talked with her recently and said, "I'm afraid we almost killed you!" She laughingly acknowledged that she was indeed quite stretched during those years.

That little blue robe with my name on the collar is gone now. But today I rejoice that my name is written in the Lamb's Book of Life. And some day I plan to sing in the celestial choir—robed in garments of white.

Thank you, Sister Ellwanger, for loving me and investing in my life.

Epilogue

Like me, my dear friend Marjorie Morgridge Weniger took piano lessons when she was young, but they never "took" with her either. So she was astonished when a young lady walked up to her one day after she had spoken to a group and said, "You were my piano teacher many years ago." Marjorie said, "I think you're mistaken. I don't even play the piano."

They reflected a little more, and finally Marjorie remembered that her longsuffering piano teacher had asked her to help some of the younger students as they came in for lessons. She had earned the grand salary of 50 cents each week!

As they laughed together, Marjorie said once again, "I just never did learn to play the piano." Her former "student" chuckled and said, "I didn't either!" Guess you can't teach what you haven't learned yourself!

Yes, it's also true that regardless of all those piano lessons that my dear daddy subsidized when I was young, I still can't play the piano. But you know what? I plan to take up the harp in heaven, and I won't even have to practice! It would be great to play a duet with David!

Recently when I was talking with my dear sister in the Lord, Barbara Stephenson, we chuckled together about our inability to play the piano. Now that she's taken up the guitar, I hope I don't have to wait until we get to heaven to hear her play!

By the way, I'll be looking for some of you other piano lesson dropouts to join me in that celestial orchestra!

She Can't Even Play the Piano!

Joyce Williams

She comes in every size and shape,
The pastor's wife, I mean.
Way too fat, or way too thin . . .
There's no place in between.

The quiet, timid ones sit back—
They don't even seem to care!
And those up-front ones are just way too loud.
They want more than their fair share.

If it's not the clothes she wears,
It's how she does her hair.
Her makeup is much too thick . . .
Makes her look like such a hick!

And those earrings that she wore last week,
Jangling and bouncing—they looked so cheap!
Like something Jezebel might wear.
I declare—it's more than I can bear.

Those kids of hers, oh, what a mess!
Always too loud—see how they dress?
What kind of mother can she be
When they act up for all to see?

And surely she could do much better
With Pastor's clothes—I'll write a letter!
His ties, his socks—they just don't match.
I tell you—she needs to get a whole new batch!

She Can't Even Play the Piano!

Last Sunday she only knew one line
Of that song we've sung time after time.
Either it's 'cause she doesn't care
Or her memory's failing her, I fear!

And that casserole that she baked
For last month's potluck dinner.
Where did she get that recipe?
It sure wasn't a winner!

I told you when they came
We were making a big mistake.
WHY, SHE CAN'T EVEN PLAY THE PIANO!
It's enough to make your heart break!

Now we only share because we care
As we sit and wonder why
We're stuck with such a pastor's wife.
It's enough to make you cry!
I JUST CAN'T BELIEVE IT—SHE CAN'T EVEN PLAY THE PIANO!

About the Contributors

Linda Armstrong and her husband, Leon, have been in ministry for more than 24 years. They crisscross the United States in a bus as itinerant evangelists, singing and preaching the gospel. Their home is the road, but they have family in North Carolina, and that's where they stay when they have some time off.

Vonette Bright and her late husband, Bill, cofounded Campus Crusade for Christ in 1951. She is an accomplished author and speaker. She is the founder of the National Prayer Committee and serves as chairwoman of the National Day of Prayer Task Force. Vonette led the way in establishing Congressional approval of the National Day of Prayer, which is observed the first Thursday in May. In 1993 she launched Women Today International. She lives in Orlando, Florida.

Jill Briscoe and her husband, Stuart, have ministered together for more than 45 years. They travel the globe sharing Jesus. They were in the states only six weeks in 2004. Jill is an active speaker and has written more than 40 books. She is executive editor of *Just Between Us*, a magazine of encouragement for ministry wives. They live in suburban Milwaukee.

Oreta Burnham and her husband, Paul, served as missionaries in the Philippines with New Tribes Mission for 34 years. They have served as teachers and church planters among the Ibaloi tribe. In recent years they have worked to translate Old Testament scriptures into the Ibaloi language. They live in Rose Hill, Kansas.

Marietta Coleman and her husband, Robert, have served in a variety of ministry assignments for more than 50 years. She has had many opportunities to mentor student ministry wives over these years. Robert is presently director of the School of Evangelism for the Billy Graham Evangelistic Association and is the distinguished professor of evangelism and discipleship at Gordon-Conwell Theological Seminary. They live in South Hamilton, Massachusetts.

Carol Cymbala and her husband, Jim, have pastored Brooklyn Tabernacle in New York City for nearly 30 years. She directs the 275-member Grammy Award-winning Brooklyn Tabernacle Choir and is a prolific songwriter. They live in New York.

Teresa Eller and her husband, Dan, have served in pastoral ministry for several years. They live in Tonganoxie, Kansas.

She Can't Even Play the Piano!

Ruth Bell Graham is the wife of Billy Graham. She was born in China to medical-missionary parents. After graduating from high school in Korea, she enrolled in Wheaton College, where she met her husband. They graduated from Wheaton and were married in 1943. She is a prolific writer and role model for women of faith. She and her husband have served together in ministry for more than 60 years. They live in Montreat, North Carolina.

Genell Johnson and her husband, Talmadge Johnson, have ministered in the Church of the Nazarene for many years. Talmadge currently serves as general superintendent for the denomination. Genell has served as district president of Nazarene Missions International and as a member of the general council of Nazarene Missions International. They live in Hermitage, Tennessee.

Patsy Lewis is a teacher, speaker, and director of women's ministries. Her ministry, Potter's Clay, reaches out to hurting people in need of encouragement to reach their potential. She and her husband, Curtis, have been in ministry for 40 years. He is district superintendent of the Kentucky District, Church of the Nazarene. They live in Louisville, Kentucky.

Beverley London and her husband, H. B., served in pastoral ministry for many years before joining Focus on the Family in 1991. She is an interior design consultant for Focus on the Family. They live in Colorado Springs.

H. B. London Jr. is vice president of church, clergy, and medical outreach for Focus on the Family. He is a fourth-generation minister who pastored for 31 years. He has served as a radio and television host and has coauthored numerous books. He operates by the slogan "God loves you as though you were the only one in all the world to love—and that makes you a very important person."

Joyce Mehl is a speaker and author. She and her late husband, Ron, worked closely together in ministry for 37 years. She continues to perpetuate their shared outreach through a radio ministry. She serves as chaplain for a children's hospital. Joyce lives in Portland, Oregon.

Pam Morgan and her husband, Larry, have served together in ministry for 32 years. She taught in public schools for a number of years. She serves as a women's ministries director in Kansas and is in demand as a speaker. She and Larry pastor in Wichita, Kansas.

Nancy Pannell and her husband, Zack, ministered together for more than 45 years. She is an author and popular speaker at family and marriage enrichment retreats. They live in Denton, Texas.

Carol Rhoads is an accomplished pianist and former teacher. Her husband, Ross, is currently chaplain of the Billy Graham Evangelistic Association, special assistant to Franklin Graham, and vice chairman of Samaritan's Purse. They live in Charlotte, North Carolina.

Joyce Rogers is a homemaker and pastor's wife. She works alongside her husband, Adrian, who pastors Bellevue Baptist Church in Memphis. Joyce is a speaker, singer, a leader of women's ministries, and an author. They live in Memphis.

Carolyn Roper and her husband, David, are codirectors of Idaho Mountain Ministries, a support and retreat ministry to pastoral couples. They began this ministry in 1995 after 34 years in local church ministry. They live in Boise, Idaho.

Frances Simpson and her husband, Eugene, pastored for 30 years, and Eugene spent their last 10 years of ministry as district superintendent for the North Carolina District, Church of the Nazarene. Frances is an author and speaker. They reside in Charlotte, North Carolina.

Kathy Slamp and her husband, David, have been in ministry for more than 35 years. They have served together around the United States in local church ministry and on college campuses. Kathy enjoys life in the parsonage and says she can't imagine any other life. She is an author and in demand as a speaker. They live in Seattle, Washington.

Linda Toler and her husband, Stan, have ministered together for more than 32 years. Linda has coauthored several books. She is active in the church they pastor, serving as women's ministries director and team teacher for the young married couples' Sunday School class. Linda has taught school for 27 years. She and Stan live in Oklahoma City.

Deletta Tompkins and her husband, Joe Lee, have been in ministry together for more than 40 years. She is a music pastor, and he is senior pastor. Deletta teaches school, gives private vocal and instrumental lessons, and directs women's ministries in her church. She and her husband live in Carthage, Missouri.

Kay Warren and her husband, Rick, started Saddleback Church with seven people in their home in southern California in 1980. With a deep desire to impact the community, the church, located in Lake Forest, California, has grown to more than 22,000 people in weekly attendance. Kay is a speaker at "purpose-driven" events and other conferences worldwide. She is the coauthor of *Foundations*, a doctrinal curriculum designed to teach the essential truths of the Christian faith. They live in California.

More Life-Changing Stories of Faith...
...From Women Just Like You!

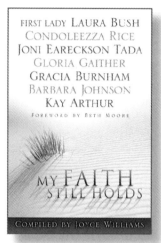

FIRST LADY LAURA BUSH
CONDOLEEZZA RICE
JONI EARECKSON TADA
GLORIA GAITHER
GRACIA BURNHAM
BARBARA JOHNSON
KAY ARTHUR
FOREWORD BY BETH MOORE

MY FAITH STILL HOLDS
COMPILED BY JOYCE WILLIAMS

083-412-078X

My Faith Still Holds

Featuring First Lady Laura Bush, Gracia Burnham, Barbara Johnson, and many others

"In hours like this, we learn that our faith is an active faith–that we are called to serve and to care for one another–and to bring hope and comfort where there is despair and sorrow."

— Laura Bush

"Faith is what gives me comfort, humility, and hope—even through the darkest hours."

—Condoleezza Rice

FOREWORD by BARBARA JOHNSON

UNSHAKABLE FAITH for SHAKY TIMES

LIZ CURTIS HIGGS · BETH MOORE
VONETTE BRIGHT · PATSY CLAIRMONT
PEGGY BENSON · and others
COMPILED by JOYCE WILLIAMS

083-412-0208

Unshakable Faith for Shaky Times

Featuring Liz Curtis Higgs, Beth Moore, Vonette Bright, Peggy Benson, Patsy Clairmont, and others

Unshakable Faith for Shaky Times is a collection of candid stories of faith from godly women around the world. Their stories challenge Christians to absolutely believe in Him in every circumstance. Through poems, prose, laughter, tears, transparency, hope, and grace, you will find absolute reliance on God scrolled across each page.

Visit your local Christian bookstore to order!